OF GRANITE
AND DREAMS

KERING

OF GRANITE
AND DREAMS
KERING

Flammarion

KER

In the Breton language, *ker* means house, home, a place to live. Thus, the name Kering is a tribute to both the origins of the Pinault family and the group, as well as a reflection of the role it plays with its brands: welcoming them, helping them grow and develop by providing all the resources they need. It also refers to the idea of "care," which is reflected in the attention Kering pays to those around it—its teams, customers, and partners— and to the future of the planet.

CONTENTS

CONQUERING
THE TIMBER MARKET
1962-90

The story of the Kering group began in 1962, when François Pinault, a young entrepreneur from Brittany, just twenty-six years old, established a small timber trading business in Rennes, France. Ambitious, driven by a strong intuition, and unafraid to take risks, he quickly stood out from his competitors. Following a period of rapid growth, Pinault SA became the leading French company in the timber industry by the late 1980s, and its founder a prominent figure on the country's economic landscape. Operating across the industry, the company acquired a number of businesses within the sector that had suffered during the crisis of the 1970s. Looking for new sources of growth, it entered the specialized distribution market, a first step toward completely changing its business model.

TRÉVÉRIEN (I.-et-V.). - Le Bourg

Top: The village of Trévérien in Brittany.
Bottom: The Breton farm where François Pinault lived until 1960.

ENTREPRENEURIAL SPIRIT (1962–64)

Rennes, France, January 2, 1962: a new company named Établissements François Pinault was born. At its head was an ambitious, determined twenty-six-year-old. In the middle of the Trente Glorieuses, this was the beginning of the story of the Kering group.

An entrepreneur's early years

François Pinault was born on August 21, 1936, in Champs-Géraux, a town of a few thousand close to Dinan, located in what is known today as the Côtes d'Armor. His father, also François, born in 1896, had a thirty-two-acre (twelve-hectare) farm six miles (ten kilometers) away, in Trévérien, a small village of just over seven hundred people, surrounded by farmland, forests, and moors. A World War I veteran, François Pinault Senior married a local woman named Eugénie Gabillard in 1932, and devoted himself to farming and logging. In addition to growing wheat, he raised around a dozen cows that provided milk and butter. He also traded in cider, which he bought from local farmers and sold as far away as Jersey and Guernsey. In 1942, he set up a sawmill on the farm, which he operated mainly during winter. With the help of a farm worker, he cut oak sleepers for the railroads, and supplied the area's carpenters and cabinetmakers. Pinault Sr. enjoyed a certain measure of affluence: he was one of the few farmers in the area to own a car and a telephone. Entrepreneurial with a gift for business, he was a respected figure. He shared little of the conservativism that characterized his region; he was interested in the modern world and was always eager to move forward. These were traits that his son would inherit.

François Pinault grew up in Trévérien, where the family moved shortly after he was born. "We lived simply. Comfort was basic, if not completely absent. There was no bathroom and no hot water. It was a bit like the nineteenth century. Despite the difficult times, we were not unhappy," the entrepreneur told his biographer, Jean Bothorel.[1] He had just turned three when World War II broke out. Then came the Battle of Sedan, the collapse of the French Army, and the capitulation. In 1940, German soldiers arrived in Trévérien. The next year, the young boy started elementary school at the public school where his father insisted on enrolling him. When not taking care of business, Pinault Sr. led clandestine missions with the Resistance.

François Pinault was nine when the war ended in 1945. After school, he would help his parents with the farm, working in the fields, taking care of the cows, churning butter, and carrying planks at the sawmill. His future seemed to be mapped out: he would take over the family enterprise. In 1947, his father agreed to enroll him at the Saint-Martin middle school in Rennes, following the advice of Mr. and Mrs. Cadiou, teachers at the school in Trévérien who saw potential in the youngster. The school was run by Eudist priests and their pupils were the progeny of the local bourgeoisie. The sons of shopkeepers and small manufacturers took classes with those of lawyers and doctors. For François Pinault, it was an immense shock. "I had tumbled into a world that was not my own. For the other students, I was a bumpkin. I was badly dressed; my French was poor: I rolled my Rs. Some memories of the humiliation I encountered are still with me," he told his other biographer, Pierre Daix.[2] He worked hard to overcome these challenges, especially to get rid of his accent. This experience would be fundamental in forging his character. His classmates' mockery stoked "a determination

1 Jean Bothorel, *François Pinault, une enfance bretonne* (Paris: Robert Laffont, 2003).

2 Pierre Daix, *François Pinault* (Paris: Éditions de Fallois, 1998).

to succeed" and the will to move forward, which would prove to be one of his strongest driving forces. It was then with no regret that, in 1952, he had to return to the family farm when his father needed his help with the sawmill. He was sixteen years old. The village where he had grown up was little changed since the 1930s, and most definitely not in the five years since he had been in Rennes. The same was not true for the rest of the country.

France and Brittany's lag

In the 1950s, France entered what would become known as the "Trente Glorieuses," the period of strong growth that lasted until the first oil crisis in 1973. The country's GDP had been growing by more than 5 percent annually since 1946, compared to an average of less than 1.2 percent during the period 1910–45. A new spirit was sweeping the nation. After years of stagnation, the birthrate was rising again. It was the age of the baby boom: between 1946 and 1968, the French population grew by more than 9 million, more than in the entire preceding century. People were living longer and infant mortality had dropped considerably.

Instigated by public authorities, major transport infrastructure projects were launched. New airports became operational, including Orly, whose first terminal opened in 1952, while the motorway network expanded at breakneck speed: between 1950 and 1970, it grew from 19 to 995 miles (30 to 1,600 kilometers). The government was also actively developing the economy, with multiple capital budget plans to ensure France's recovery: in the housing sector, for example, thousands of new buildings featuring every modern comfort—notably running water and electricity—were under construction, along with a nuclear program made tangible in 1955 with the commissioning of the Marcoule plutonium plant.

The changes in the country's industry were immense. Stimulated by low energy prices—the price of a barrel of oil remained at around three dollars until the 1970s—strong demand, the proliferation of information technology, and the spread of American production methods—most notably Fordism—companies experienced spectacular gains in productivity. Industry had entered the age of mass production, making it possible to continually produce more at ever-lower costs. The very structure of the economy was changing: in 1955, the primary sector—agriculture, fishing, and mining—represented 36 percent of the active population, but in 1973, the figure was hardly more than 10 percent, due to the rural exodus and the transition to large-scale industrial farming. During the same period, the secondary sector accounted for 32 to 38 percent of the workforce and the burgeoning tertiary sector grew from 32 to 51 percent.

Modernization was sweeping the country, dramatically changing the lives of French people. It was an era of full employment, rising salaries, and increased mass consumption, made possible by the transformation of production systems. By the mid-1950s, the "American way of life" had reached every level of French society: more households had an electric stove, a refrigerator, a washing machine, a dishwasher, or even one of the new food processors that were making the fortunes of certain manufacturers, including Jean Mantelet, founder of Moulinex. Household appliance use was 3 percent in 1950; in 1965, it had grown to 20 percent, and to 57 percent in the early 1970s. Increasing numbers of French people owned a car. By the end of the 1960s, one household in two owned one. Compare this to only 14 percent in 1950. A true "car culture" flourished throughout the country, leading to new kinds of settlements—residential suburbs—and new businesses—first supermarkets, and then hypermarkets.

In the space of barely thirty years, society had entered modern life. What a contrast with Brittany, which was still lagging behind the rest of the country in the 1950s. The primary sector continued to dominate—accounting for more than 50 percent of the workforce compared to 36 percent for France as a whole—and the population was predominantly rural—70 percent as opposed to the country's overall rate of 46 percent. Small and without sufficient mechanization, farms turned little profit. As for manufacturing, it represented only 20 percent of workers, compared to 32 percent for France as a whole. Most of these were very small companies, managed using traditional methods and with very little interest in growing. Once known for its factories, the region had been emptied of its industries throughout the nineteenth century because of competition from other areas in France. In Brittany, wealth became tied primarily to real estate, thus depriving the region of entrepreneurs and capital. Infrastructure languished in a similar way. In the mid-1950s, the region lacked major roads. It was not until 1968, that a "road plan" was launched to open up the region. This resulted in the construction, beginning in 1970, of the expressway linking Brest to Rennes, via Morlaix and Guingamp, and to Nantes, via Lorient and Vannes. Air links were not any better. There were three airports—Brest, Quimper, and Rennes. But it was not until the 1960s, even the early 1970s, that the first commercial air links with Paris were established.

Poorly connected to the rest of the country, Brittany lived closed in on itself. Daily life was austere. In the mid-1950s, nearly 80 percent of rural homes still did not have running water—as opposed to 30 percent for France as a whole. Half of rural communities were not yet electrified, a much higher percentage than the rest of the country. But things were beginning to change. In 1950, at the initiative of elected officials and business leaders, the Breton liaison committee CELIB (Comité d'étude et de liaison des intérêts bretons) was created, with the goal of promoting Brittany's economic development and identity. The group was behind the 1968 road plan. In the countryside, a new generation of farmers was working to implement modern agriculture. Even more ambitious, certain food industrialists began conquering the immense Parisian market. But these initiatives did not see any real results until the 1960s. In many ways, François Pinault's career is representative of Brittany's "awakening" and the emergence of a new generation of entrepreneurs determined to move beyond their natal region. For the time being, though, it was on the family farm, to which he returned in 1952, that his destiny had long been foretold.

Early experiences

At the farm in Trévérien, nothing seemed to have really changed since the end of the war. Pinault Sr. continued running his farm and operating the sawmill in parallel. This is where François Pinault spent his days, "cutting down trees, sawing them, felling them, not always with a chainsaw," as he told Pierre Daix. In order to perfect his knowledge, the young man even enrolled in the Lycée des Métiers du Bois in Luchon, in the Pyrénées, a

professional school dedicated to woodworking trades. He only stayed at the wood school for a few days, the time it took for him to realize that he knew more about the subject than his teachers.

Relations between François and his father soon became heated. It was a question of temperament: both had strong characters. It was also a question of vision: the young man was convinced that the sawmill had to be modernized—and told his father so—to expand not just its clientele but also its sources of timber, as Tréverien did not have enough forests to allow any evolution in scale. Already there was the ambition and desire to grow. Later, François Pinault would come to understand how to put such plans into action. But his father would hear nothing of it. At fifty-six, this proud, hardworking farmer, whose legendary energy had become a little dulled over time, had no intention of questioning a model that perfectly suited his needs. One day in 1956, after a discussion that was a little more turbulent than usual, François Pinault decided to leave his father's farm and try his hand elsewhere. He was not yet twenty years old. However, he had to free himself from one last constraint: compulsory military service. He was still too young, but he could preempt the conscription on the condition that he go to Algeria. This is what he chose to do.

The French Army had been waging war in Algeria since 1954. France had been present in the country since conquering it in 1830; on November 1, 1954, an uprising erupted. More than 300,000 French soldiers were already stationed in the region. François Pinault arrived in Algeria in the early summer of 1956. The experience was completely new for him; he had never before left his native Brittany. During his thirty months of military service, he rubbed shoulders with young people from all walks of life, discovered another culture, and was confronted with the horrors of war every day. When he returned to France in late 1958 with nothing in his bag but the Cross for Military Valor, it was to resume the routine of Tréverien and the family farm, and to once again go head-to-head with his father, with whom tensions quickly flared. But, sadly, not for very long: in September 1959, Pinault Sr. was stung by a hornet and died suddenly. For his son, it was time to make a choice: in agreement with his brother and two sisters, he decided to close the sawmill and sell the timber stock. He found himself a job with the timber trading firm Gautier Frères, a company that his father had established good relations with, which also operated a large sawmill in Rennes. The company's leader Baptiste Gautier had just lost his brother and it was as a partner as much as a manager that François Pinault joined the company. In 1960, he married Baptiste's only daughter, Louisette, with whom he would have three children.

François Pinault remained with Gautier Frères for two years. During this time, he was responsible for purchasing the standing timber, helping in the sawmill, and selling planks. Within six months, he had doubled the sawmill's turnover. He was also charged with selling a piece of land owned by the Gautier family and coveted by the Mutuelles du Mans insurance company. He sold it for four times the expected price, evidence of his formidable negotiating skills. François Pinault's future seemed set: he would take over the family business or, alternatively, go and make a career elsewhere. But he had other plans. As he approached his twenty-fifth birthday, his intention was to set up his own business. He had been considering this course for years, since his schooldays, when he was taunted by his classmates at Saint-Martin middle school in Rennes. It was then that he promised himself to never depend on anyone.

And so on January 2, 1962, with the help of his father-in-law and two of his uncles, who lent him 600,000 francs—a sum that he repaid in full—François Pinault created a sole proprietorship in Rennes, Établissements François Pinault. The young entrepreneur did not take this leap empty-handed. Through the years spent working with his father in the family's small sawmill and then at Gautier Frères, he had a solid foundation in the timber market. From purchasing wood to cutting planks, he had mastered every stage. From his father, with whom he had so often clashed, he learned to be rigorous—a rigor he applied to himself and others—to remain extremely vigilant and to never rest on his laurels. Ambitious and determined, he was willing to take risks to succeed, even if it meant upending the way things had usually been done. This is exactly what he would do, and how he would launch an astonishing entrepreneurial adventure.

Early days in the timber trade

Located on Rue de la Roberdière, on the road to Lorient in the industrial zone just outside Rennes, the young company specialized in timber trading, a sector that its founder, as already noted, knew inside out: it purchased softwoods for lumber that it sold to carpenters and cabinetmakers. Its resources were modest. In addition to six employees—including a truck driver, three workers, and a receptionist/typist to type up the orders and deliveries—there was the warehouse François Pinault had built and one or two trucks that were painted pastis yellow to make sure they stood out. A low-cost publicity strategy that speaks volumes about his ambitions: the young entrepreneur had decided to conquer the market.

The timing was particularly good. Since the mid-1950s, housing had been a priority for the government. Vast construction programs were launched and such initiatives continued at an accelerated pace in the 1960s and 1970s. The figures tell the story: in 1953, less than 100,000 new residences were built in France; in 1960, that number was 320,000, rising to 410,000 in 1965, and to 550,000 in 1971! Urban centers were being renewed, large housing projects were developed, suburbs were expanding on a massive scale, and these suburban areas were being filled with houses. In some fifteen years, France's urban landscape had been totally transformed. Brittany was not left behind, starting with its capital, Rennes. From the early 1960s, the city underwent immense changes. To accommodate a population that was rapidly growing thanks to the rural exodus and the thousands of workers at the Citroën La Janais factory—opened in 1960— new constructions mushroomed.

When he embarked on his entrepreneurial venture, François Pinault was therefore confident that he would have enough work. The new houses being built in and around Rennes needed timber for windows, doors, closets, and partitions. But there was plenty of competition. In the early 1960s, Brittany had hundreds of timber trading companies. Most were small, family-run businesses operating locally. The region was well-stocked with sawmills—nearly a thousand of the 15,000 then operating in France. A small town like Querrien, near Quimperlé (population 2,700 in 1962), had at least four. Operating at a level above these traders and small manufacturers were the timber industry's aristocracy: the importers. They supplied the material to the trading companies, the wholesalers, and the sawmills. Their main

ANNÉE.	CONTENANCE.			REVENU bâti, non bâti.		COMPTES RATTACHÉS.						REVENU TOTAL (col. 3 + 5 + 7) bâti, non bâti.	
						NUMÉRO.	REVENU bâti, non bâti.		NUMÉRO.	REVENU bâti, non bâti.			
1	ha.	a.	ca.	NF.	c.	4	NF.	c.	6	NF.	c.	NF.	c.
19		89	76	102	03								
1963				64	23								
1964		89	86										
1965		89	86	262	75								
1968	1	33	68	21	03								
1969	1	33	68	306	55								
19													

Pour 19 63. *Pinault François époux Texier Gautier* 35 bis Rue Legraverend
96 Rue au Lorient.

PROPRIÉTÉS BATIES.

MUTATIONS.				DÉSIGNATION DES PROPRIÉTÉS.				REVENU (Revision 1943).					REVENU (Revision 19___).					REVENU (Revision 19___).					
ENTRÉE.		SORTIE.		SECTION.	NUMÉRO DU PLAN.	LIEUDIT ou RUE ET NUMÉRO.	NATURE DE LA PROPRIÉTÉ (1).	MAI-SONS.	USINES.			TOTAL.	MAI-SONS.	USINES.			TOTAL.	MAI-SONS.	USINES.			TOTAL.	
ANNÉE.	TIRÉ DE	ANNÉE.	PORTÉ A						BÂTI-MENTS.	OUTIL-LAGE.				BÂTI-MENTS.	OUTIL-LAGE.				BÂTI-MENTS.	OUTIL-LAGE.		
1	2	3	4	5	6	7	8	9	10	11	12		13	14	15	16		17	18	19	20	21
								fr.	fr.	fr.	fr.											
1965	CN 1964	1970	652	E	219/314	Rue de la Roberdière Rte de Lorient	Dépôt ouvert	26.275			26.275											CN 1962 repris 1965 + AC 1964 N 9. E 229 2
1969	C N 1968			E	291 292/314	rue de la Roberdière	dépôt non couvert	4.380			4.380											oy. VI.
1970	652			E	293/314	rue de la Roberdière n° 4	dépôt (bureau)	28.305			28.305											

30.655

(1) Ainsi que le numéro du lot et la quote-part dans la propriété du sol lorsqu'il a été établi un état descriptif de division.

Imprimeries Oberthur - Rennes.

Records relating to the first premises occupied by
Établissements François Pinault, on Rue de la Roberdière in Rennes.

NUMÉRO DES MAISONS	DESIGNATION et adresse (lieu-dit ou rue et n°) des contribuables (1)	NOMBRE DE PERSONNES A CHARGE	CONTRIBUTION MOBILIÈRE — 1re ligne : Loyer matriciel brut / 2e ligne : Abattements / 3e ligne : Loyer matriciel imposable	TAXE D'HABITATION — 1re ligne : Valeur locative réelle / 2e ligne : Abattements / 3e ligne : Valeur locative imposable	CONTRIBUTION DES PATENTES — DÉSIGNATION DES PROFESSIONS — Eléments du droit fixe et indications diverses	Mention du tabl. A (et de la classe), du tabl. B ou du tabl. C (partie et groupe)	DROIT FIXE — MONTANT des droits résultant de l'application du tarif
1	Art. 170450 M Pinault François	3	F c	F c	Marchand de bois pour la construction et l'industrie vendant qu'aux entrepreneur ou particuliers Taxe déterminée 0,65 52 salariés 0,325 = 16,90	A3	17 55
	Art. 170451 M Trogerais Alphonse	1	5 00 / 1 30 / 3 70	64 00 / 16 / 48			
	Art. 170452 M S.A.R.L France Bois 34 Rue Amiral Courbet				Marchand de bois pour la construction ou l'industrie vendant qu'aux entrepreneur ou particuliers Taxe déterminée 0,65 3 salariés 0,325 = 0,975	B3	162 50
	Art. 170457 M S.A.R.L Meiss et Sodima		Rue Manoir de Servigné		Marchand de produits de quincaillerie en detail n'occupant pas plus de 30 salariés Marchand de carburants ou combustibles liquides I.M.E Taxe déterminée 0,65 2 1 salarié 0,325 6,825 2 à 0,275 = 0,55	A3 / I74	8 02 50
	Art. 170458 M Chantreux Lucien 27 Square Charles Dublin - Rennes				Tôlier réparateur Réduction 15% Taxe déterminée 0,45 1 salarié 0,10 = 0,10	A5	0 55
	Art. 170459 M S.N.C Guérard et Parnole				Entrepositaire de marchandises Taxe déterminée 0,65 4 salariés 0,325 = 1,30	B3	1 95

source was Scandinavia, supplier of most of France's timber. The importers were part of the all-powerful Fédération Française des Importateurs de Bois du Nord—the "Fédé" as it was called—and could be found operating in all of Brittany's ports, from Saint-Malo to Nantes. Their monopoly meant they negotiated directly with Finnish and Swedish exporters, set prices, and determined import quantities. Their closed system dominated all the other stakeholders in the network.

With a handful of employees, a warehouse, and a few trucks, Établissements François Pinault seemed indistinguishable from the many other small timber trading companies in Brittany at the time, which were also looking to profit from the opportunities presented by the major construction programs. Was nothing different? There was something, in fact. Even at the time of its creation, the small enterprise stood apart thanks to its assertive approach to trade. "I had no choice: I had no cash flow and every day I had to find new clients," François Pinault told Jean Bothorel. To manage the challenges, the entrepreneur fought on all fronts. He started each day at 5:00 a.m., often working eighteen hours per day and demanding that his staff give their best. He was always watchful, negotiating reductions with suppliers to offer his clients better deals, constantly expanding his range of products, and emphasizing quality and service. Company schedules were adjusted to ensure faster delivery at more regular intervals. A preordering system was also established, meaning that timber could be purchased in larger quantities, and thus at better prices. In the timber industry, where people were generally more concerned with defending their positions as opposed to conquering new ones, such practices were not widespread. Though he had not yet shaken up the sector—that time would come soon enough—he had already begun to attack his competitors head-on with determination. In Rennes and the surrounding areas, however, few people paid attention to the small business. By the time they did, it would be too late.

No matter, the results were there: in the first year, Établissements François Pinault's revenue reached 600,000 francs; in 1963, it rose to 2.5 million francs, and to 3.4 million the following year. The company was profitable from the outset. But success had its downside. "The more my sales volume grew, the more the Fédération des Importateurs set prices that left me with almost no margin. I quickly realized that I had no choice: import timber directly from the north or fold," François Pinault recounts in his biography by Jean Bothorel. Two years after launching his business, the young entrepreneur was about to take on substantial risks in order to challenge the rules that were controlling the sector.

Construction of the Colombier district in Rennes, c. 1975.

Ets François PINAULT

BOIS et PANNEAUX

ZONE INDUSTRIELLE - **RENNES** - Tél. **40.69.06** et **07**

Célamine

LAMIFIÉ INTÉGRAL

Contreplaqués et Spécialités
MULTIPLEX

— Panneaux agglomérés

— Panneaux de Fibres

Parquets mosaïques et traditionnels - Moulures, etc...

Advertising published in the *Ouest-France* daily newspaper.

A LA FOIRE DE RENNES, au stand n° 39

LES ÉTABLISSEMENTS PINAULT
(bois et panneaux)

route de Lorient, à RENNES, présentent :

Établissements François Pinault participated in the 1962 Rennes fair.

Pages 24-25: Log driving in Sweden in 1969.
Above: François Pinault and his site foreman on the docks of Saint-Malo in 1965.

DARING AND RISK (1965–78)

In October 1964, François Pinault and a colleague left France for a two-week trip to Sweden and then Finland, with the intention of buying timber directly. Thus began the "timber war," which would transform his company's future.

The "timber war"

In deciding to buy timber at the source, François Pinault had one objective: to bypass the middlemen on which the French timber industry was established. In the early 1960s, the import chain of Scandinavian timber had three main stages. First, Swedish and Finnish sawmills sold their wood through a local broker who charged a fee of around 2.5 percent. This broker would then contact a French counterpart who would in turn sell the consignment to importers for a further 2.5 percent commission. Finally, the importers resold the goods to French traders, adding a sizeable margin in the process. Thus, at every stage, the cost of timber exported from Scandinavia grew, and these considerable additions were borne by the merchants at the end of the chain, like François Pinault, leaving them with very little profit. This system was hindering his growth and the entrepreneur's intention was to break it. His goal wasn't to work with a specific intermediary but to circumvent them all: the broker in Scandinavia, his contact in France, and the "Fédé" importers. In doing this, François Pinault was taking on considerable risk, setting against him all those whose livelihoods came from importing wood — and with whose interests he was going to clash head-on, exposing himself, inevitably, to retaliation. The danger was real: as a newcomer to the profession, at the head of a small company with few resources, François Pinault had little clout against the well-established middlemen. He could only rely on himself: no one had ever dared take on the "Fédération," the importers' powerful trade association. François Pinault was alone: if he failed, he would probably not be able to continue buying timber, or else under such conditions that it would mean the end of his entrepreneurial adventure.

But this was not the only risk that François Pinault was taking. Bypassing the traditional intermediaries would force him to completely revise his model. Up until then, one or two trucks had been enough for his orders; from now on, he would have to load an entire ship, a hundred times more! In addition, he would need to pay for the goods and shipping in advance. For a company with no cash flow, this was a real challenge. And, finally, he had to source new clients to buy the huge quantity of timber he was planning to import from Scandinavia. Open warfare with importers, the need to change scale, to find money, to secure new customers... There were a lot of challenges for a company of just ten people.

François Pinault carefully prepared his venture. His first success was attracting several of his customers to join the enterprise: enticed by the advantageous prices the young entrepreneur was offering, they agreed to order and pay for large quantities of timber in advance. Encouraged by those strong connections, the young entrepreneur then managed to convince his banker, Roger Puéchaldou, head of the Crédit Lyonnais branch in Rennes, to extend a loan to finance the acquisition of the timber and to charter the ship, with interest accruing until the cargo was unloaded. There was a new risk on the horizon: that the ship would be delayed for one reason or another—the weather, technical problems, or such—and the entire enterprise would be faced with considerable additional costs. Finally, to stack the odds in his favor, François Pinault decided to travel to Scandinavia with one of his employees, Raymond Masson, who had only recently joined the company. Previously with the Société Commerciale d'Affrètement et de Combustibles (SCAC), which had a major wood importing subsidiary, he knew the import routes and already had some contacts on the ground. In the first months of 1964, everything was in place, but nothing was guaranteed. There was no certainty that the Scandinavian forestry operators would agree to negotiate with the French entrepreneur and, if they did, that the transport would go smoothly. The risks were considerable. François Pinault was playing a high-stakes game.

When the entrepreneur and his colleague arrived in Scandinavia in October 1964, things started well. They had chosen their contacts carefully. "Because the big loggers were already connected to importers, we met with the small ones, those who had no exterior markets. We were offering them a new outlet. They were extremely interested," François Pinault told Pierre Daix. Several export contracts were signed with mid-sized Swedish and Finnish sawmills. This was a remarkable achievement, even more so because neither François Pinault nor Raymond Masson spoke English.

The subsequent operations, though, proved more difficult. The ship charted by Établissements François Pinault, which was to leave from a Finnish port for unloading in Saint-Malo, was blocked in Germany's Kiel Canal because of a cold snap across Europe. This was bad news for the entrepreneur, whose interest rates would automatically increase until unloading, and who would have to explain to clients who trusted him to deliver on time that their supplies would arrive late. But that wasn't all! The Fédération Française des Importateurs de Bois knew what François Pinault was doing. It was determined to break the back of this entrepreneur who had come from nowhere and who had the audacity to attack head-on. Nothing could be easier: all it had to do was to put pressure on the Saint-Malo dockworkers to ensure they would not unload his ship when it arrived in port. This time the threat was even more serious: if the goods were not unloaded, the entire system devised by François Pinault would collapse and his clients would turn to his competitors, those who worked with the "Fédé," to order timber. The entrepreneur hurried to the docks and after much discussion, he reached an arrangement with the longshoremen: they would not unload the ship but would turn a blind eye if he brought in his own team. This was an unprecedented shift from the dockers' monopoly on the ports. The result saved François Pinault from the disaster that everyone was expecting.

The rest of the story has become legendary. Within hours of this agreement, the entrepreneur contacted each of the clients who had agreed to order timber in advance to secure their help in unloading the ship. Almost all agreed to "lend" some staff. In the first days of 1965, around sixty people—including, of course, François Pinault himself and all his staff—met on the docks of Saint-Malo to unload, by hand, the holds of the ship. The operation took two or three days. François Pinault had won his bet: he had successfully eliminated the middlemen who were corrupting the industry and impeding his own expansion. He was the first to have done it, showing extraordinary audacity and self-confidence. The system's very foundation had been rocked. The unloading of that first ship on the docks of Saint-Malo was not the end of the war between François Pinault and the Fédération des Importateurs. It would continue for years to come. Decidedly overconfident, the importers continued to regard the young entrepreneur with

The port of Saint-Malo in 1968.

Unloading planks of Swedish pine in Saint-Malo in the 1980s.

disdain: they did not take him seriously and regularly predicted his downfall. "Too ambitious, in too much of a hurry: he won't last long," they said. The future would prove them wrong. The other trading houses stuck with the old system, which for many of them would lead to their demise. But none of that mattered to François Pinault: three years after creating his company, he had the means to move forward. Shortly after the arrival of the first shipment, he launched the subsidiary France-Bois, which would handle importing timber from Scandinavia. From that perspective, 1965 was a pivotal year in the company's history, the year when everything really began, as its leader himself acknowledges. The time to fly had come.

Flying high

With the arrival of the first ship in Saint-Malo, Établissements François Pinault entered a new era. Between March 1965 and summer 1966, no less than thirty ships arrived from Scandinavia, twice as many as Sogebois, one of France's largest timber importers. A virtuous circle had been established: free of middlemen, François Pinault was able to acquire large quantities of wood in Finland and Sweden at a good price, which he then resold in France at prices below any competitor, enabling him to expand and grow customer loyalty. What François Pinault actually invented in the mid-1960s was the broadening, or "massification," of the timber market, based on a model that already existed elsewhere, particularly in the consumer goods sector.

This strategy's effectiveness was strengthened because it was underpinned by unremitting urban proliferation and by the expansion of agriculture. In the second half of the 1960s, Rennes was growing by more than three thousand new residents per year, while Brittany's countryside was covered with new buildings: farm buildings and industrial livestock shelters, as well as factories and companies specializing in the processing of agricultural raw materials and animal products. This dual urban and rural evolution boosted not only the construction sector but also suppliers, including François Pinault. The young entrepreneur was the first in the timber industry to take note of the significant transformations happening all around him and to understand the opportunities they offered to the most daring. In his opinion, the days of small ambitions, of keeping to yourself, of limited horizons, were over: big thinking was required, and going beyond your own territory was essential, even if it meant challenging entrenched positions, as he already had done. Along with a few others—including Daniel Roullier with fertilizers and animal feed; Pierre Doux, Jean Guyomarc'h, and Jacques Tilly with poultry; and Émile Bridel in dairy products—François Pinault was one of the pioneers of the "Breton miracle." Some of these trailblazers belonged to the Club des Trente, a think tank created in 1973 by a few Breton entrepreneurs determined to further development in the region.

Meanwhile, François Pinault was responding to market expansion on every front, to better serve, more quickly and at less cost, the growing number of clients who had placed their trust in him. He was acutely aware of one issue: timber handling. The loading and unloading of timber—sawn, unplaned wood planks—had always been done manually, piece by piece. These operations were therefore long and, above all, expensive: ships had to be docked for several days while their holds were emptied, increasing port costs and reducing the number of shipments. No one had previously questioned these practices. François Pinault, however, did not hesitate. To optimize handling, he had the idea of grouping the timber together, in bundles—"pallets"—fixed by cables. But for the system to be truly efficient, the boards had to be uniform, which was far from being the case. They were neither the same size nor the same thickness. This lack of standardization made it difficult to transport and store the boards. However, in Scandinavia, where he returned in 1965, François Pinault convinced certain suppliers to standardize their wood panels. Others followed in quick succession. All that remained was to invest in modern handling equipment—elevator trucks, cranes, and so on—and to negotiate fiercely with the dockworkers, who were not pleased with these innovations, which could potentially reduce their workload. The negotiations were short and tough. The dockworkers only gave in when François Pinault convinced them that the reduction in the number of longshoremen assigned to unloading a ship would be offset, to a large extent, by the acceleration in rotations. The result of these innovations was spectacular: in Saint-Malo, the unloading time for ships dropped from an average of three or four days to one day. The operation now only required an average of seven or eight workers, compared to around thirty previously. But the number of ships able to dock tripled. The result was a considerable reduction in costs, which François Pinault quickly passed on to his clients.

Carried out in parallel to the elimination of the middlemen, this double revolution, the pallet and standardization, completed the overhaul of the methods that had governed the timber industry for years, giving Établissements François Pinault a significant lead over other trading companies. In 1966, the company's revenue reached 15 million francs, that is, twenty-five times that of 1962! In full expansion, the company remained modest. In 1966, along with France-Bois, its subsidiary dedicated to importing timber, it had only eighteen employees. François Pinault expected them to be available any time, even outside working hours. But at the same time, they were given autonomy, able to take initiative and be on the lookout for any opportunities that might appear. In comparison to its competitors who were more conventional, the small company was characterized by a distinctive approach to its operations: "commando mode." It was about acting fast, not wasting time, being fully committed to work, and being reactive. François Pinault led by example: everywhere at once, crisscrossing the region to meet clients or potential contacts, inspecting timber stocks, or organizing the unloading of a ship, he worked seven days a week, utilizing Sundays to revise the company's accounts, call buyers, and think about new initiatives.

Of course, there were always new initiatives. At the end of the 1960s, the entrepreneur had a new idea: having eliminated most of the middlemen and revolutionized handling, he intended to broaden his horizons far beyond trade and position his company at every level of the wood industry, from industrial processing to distribution. Once again, François Pinault was preparing to revolutionize the industry.

Successfully gambling on vertical integration

At the very end of 1969, François Pinault acquired a four-hectare parcel of land in Saint-Malo, in the new industrial zone nearby the Rance Tidal Power

A carpentry workshop in Rennes.

Station. He immediately built a sawing and planing center on the site. Here, the unprocessed timber from Scandinavia would be transformed, cut to size to meet customers' specific needs. With this new facility, the company made a dramatic entry into the industry; the center's creation caught its attention. Établissements François Pinault was not the first trading company to enter the business of wood processing, of course; many of its competitors had sawmills, sometimes long established. But compared to them, the company was, yet again, distinguished by its dynamism and its commitment to exploring and conquering new markets. Nothing at the Saint-Malo site was wasted. On the contrary, everything was used! Rather than being thrown away, offcuts were used to make paneling, parquet flooring, garden beds, and even litter for animals. Recycling before its time? Perhaps. But above all, a pragmatic approach that pushed the company to constantly expand the range of products it offered clients. This was undoubtedly the real originality of the company François Pinault founded.

In 1970, the entrepreneur opened a second industrial center, close to Nantes. But he did not stop there. His new mission was to move into distribution. The principle remained the same: a question of working without intermediaries. In this instance, he had the wholesalers—who made up the bulk of the company's clients—in his sights. They naturally added a margin to the wood Établissements François Pinault supplied them with and which they then resold to manufacturers and craftsmen. By delivering directly to the latter, the company would be able to control its sales and recuperate these margins for itself, while simultaneously passing on always more attractive prices to its end customers. It would also be less vulnerable in the event of poor sales or an economic downturn. The timber industry had never seen such a vertical integration strategy: no company had positioned itself across the entire sector, from trading the raw material to distribution. It was not, however, without risk: like the battle with the importers, it would inevitably lead to conflict with the resellers. As an excellent reader of his market, François Pinault had no doubt that manufacturers and craftsmen, attracted by the competitive pricing, would continue to work directly with him.

Between 1969 and 1972, three agencies were opened in Rennes, Saint-Malo, and Nantes. Just ten years after its creation, the company had established itself as truly regional. Its revenue also increased significantly. Between 1968 and 1972, it rose from 25 to 163 million francs. The sites in Rennes, Saint-Malo, Nantes, and Quimper now employed sixty-three people. The warehouses, agencies, and industrial woodworking facilities were in perfect shape. This was the result of the initiatives undertaken by Hubert Guidal, former head of production at Sogebois, who was recruited in 1970. Immediately on his arrival, he suggested to François Pinault that they put some sorely needed order into the work sites. After initially doubting the advantage of such an approach—"Why put away timber that is going to be delivered to the customer in one or two days?" François Pinault asked him, a little skeptical—the boss let himself be convinced that an orderly site would help the company's image and facilitate the handling operations.

In 1970, recognizing his company's change in scale, but also to simplify its structure, François Pinault merged Établissements François Pinault with its subsidiary, France-Bois. Pinault France was born. The new company's logo was in the shape of a circle representing the Earth, from which an arrow emerges, a symbol of going beyond. The company's new name drew sarcastic comments from within the industry. "Why not Pinault-Europe or Pinault-Monde!" laughed the members of the Fédération, who had not recovered from losing their monopoly on importing Scandinavian wood. "It was a bit pretentious, I admit, but it clearly announced my direction," explains François Pinault in Pierre Daix's book. Indeed, the name Pinault France says a lot about the entrepreneur's ambition. After Brittany it would, in fact, be France, then Europe, and the world.

In his native region, François Pinault was increasingly in the news. The "timber war" he had won against the importers, the technical innovations he implemented for handling lumber in Saint-Malo, his vertical integration strategy, and the drastic reduction in prices that these innovations had brought about, drew a number of comments—generally not very friendly—but also concern: unable to adapt, many traders closed or were on the verge of doing so. In 1972, the recruitment of Jean Leprince as his "right-hand man" brought fresh commentary. An agricultural engineer, he had previously headed the dairy department of the Coopérative des Agriculteurs de Landerneau, the region's largest milk producer. A veritable Breton institution! His arrival at Pinault France, a small business, still relatively unknown, was a bombshell in business circles: they suddenly discovered this young entrepreneur, always in a hurry, who in only a few years, had become one of France's major timber importers. Particularly surprising to the business world was François Pinault's small plane that he frequently traveled on: such a "luxury" was not yet commonplace. However, it says a lot about François Pinault's ambition and his desire to stay one step ahead of his competitors. After long ignoring them—for lack of time as much as for lack of interest—François Pinault began forging links with the region's economic stakeholders. Especially with the Junior Chamber of Commerce, of which he was a member. He also became friends with Michel Giraud, who had begun importing exotic wood and who launched a political career in 1971 that would ultimately lead him to the Senate, the National Assembly, and to the head of several ministries. François Pinault and his new wife Maryvonne Campbell—he and Louisette Gautier divorced in 1965—entertained friends and relatives at La Droulinais, the property he purchased in 1971. Now well established in Brittany, François Pinault's reputation had spread internationally. And it was from abroad that he received, in late 1972, an unexpected proposal.

A change of scale

In December 1972, François Pinault met with the Managing Director of Luterma-France, a subsidiary of the British group Venesta International, in Rennes. Initially specializing in the production of plastic and polystyrene products, the group had recently diversified into plywood production, to take advantage of the construction boom. This is why it had acquired Luterma, the Estonian pioneer of plywood furniture. Venesta had also taken over several wood merchants throughout France. Its strategy was clear: the British group wanted to expand its distribution by utilizing already well-established companies. From this perspective, the acquisition of Pinault France, well positioned in Brittany and with its own distribution network, would be a major breakthrough. Hence the visit to Rennes by Luterma's Managing Director, who arrived with a proposition for François Pinault: to buy his company.

"I was a bit surprised at first. I didn't think that this kind of business could be sold. But the British were so insistent that I finally said yes," François Pinault recounts today. But he wasn't going to accept just any price. Not being the buyer this time, he set the bar very high, convinced that the deal would end there. To his great surprise, the British didn't negotiate: they agreed to 25 million francs for an 80 percent stake in Pinault France, with its founder maintaining the other 20 percent. And in addition, they asked François Pinault to remain at the head of the company for two years. The transaction was finalized on March 31, 1973. Naturally, it caused great commotion across the industry. For many of his competitors, it sounded the death knell of François Pinault, the haughty entrepreneur who had believed he could stand alone against the entire industry. No one imagined, even for a moment, that through selling his company he was, on the contrary, arming himself—considering his limited resources—with the means to accelerate his company's growth. As he explained to colleagues who were concerned about the future: "What I imagined I could do with you and my own funds, we can achieve more quickly and with better resources," he said.

And that is exactly what happened! Thanks to Venesta's money, Pinault France was able to rapidly expand its distribution network. Between April and May 1973, no less than nine agencies were opened, in Saint-Brieuc, Morlaix, Quimper, Vannes, and Cholet, as well as Redon, Laval, Pontivy, and La Roche-sur-Yon. Pinault France was now operating throughout Brittany and in neighboring departments. This accomplished the work of eliminating the last middlemen—the retailers—which had begun four years earlier. In the wake of such growth, the number of employees jumped: in 1973, there were 148. Revenue also increased, to 300 million francs. François Pinault and the small team supporting him—Jean Leprince in general management, Hubert Guidal in operations, Jean-Pierre Andrevon in finance, and Jean-Rémy Jacquemin in sales—faced challenges in managing the company's growth. But they remained agile, flexible, and responsive, acting in the same way the company had always done. This was in stark contrast to Venesta, whose way of operating was far more bureaucratic, and thus moved slowly. In mid-fall 1973, it seemed as if nothing could interrupt the small company's intensely rapid development. On Route de Saint-Brieuc, in the Pacé industrial zone on the outskirts of Rennes, where Pinault France had just moved its head office, the mood was optimistic; there was a spirit of conquest in the air. But then something happened that threw everything into question.

Crisis and revival

That something was the first oil crisis. On October 13, 1973, in order to sanction Western countries for their support of Israel in its war with Egypt and Syria, the Organization of Petroleum Exporting Countries (OPEC) imposed an embargo, which doubled the price of black gold. Two months later, a further increase followed. In the space of a few weeks, oil prices rose from 2.59 to 11.65 US dollars per barrel. The shock for industrialized countries, whose growth since the end of the Second World War was based on abundant, cheap oil, was immense. With this first oil crisis—a second followed in 1979—the "Trente Glorieuses," the thirty years of economic prosperity that had begun in 1945, came to an end. A new era began, characterized by inflation, recession, and unemployment. Industrial production in France dropped 12 percent between 1974 and 1975.

The crisis affected every industry and every company. Pinault France felt the effects in spring 1974. Construction sites throughout France were shut down or put on hiatus in hopes of better days. Without orders, construction companies, carpenters, and joiners stopped buying wood. The collapse of the market hit the company hard. The situation was exacerbated by the fact that in summer 1973, it had ordered large quantities of timber to supply its new branches. With no orders, the stock sat on the Saint-Malo docks and in warehouses. The result: revenue fell almost 35 percent between 1973 and 1974. But that wasn't all! In the middle of the financial and stock market slump, Venesta International was no longer able to finance its subsidiary's investments or the capital injection it had committed to. "Every day, the company was losing money. This had never happened to me before. We were virtually bankrupt, and the British were telling us to sort it out. I had two options: wash my hands of everything and retreat, or to look for a way out that would safeguard my employees and ensure that my unpaid suppliers got part of their investment back," François Pinault would later tell Jean Bothorel. The entrepreneur chose the second course of action. In fall 1974, he made his decision: he would buy back the company he had created.

Luckily, he had the resources. A few months earlier, in June 1974, he had invested a small percentage of the money he had received from Venesta for the sale of Pinault France—300,000 francs—on the stock market, in sugar futures. The entrepreneur knew nothing of such investment. He ventured into it in hopes of recouping the losses he had suffered on the stock market in the wake of the first oil crisis. But thanks to a little flair, luck smiled on him: at the end of 1974, rumors of a shortage drove sugar prices to new heights. At the time he wisely decided to withdraw, François Pinault had made 10 million francs. He would never again resort to such speculation. But the capital gain gave him the means to negotiate with Venesta.

The discussions would be long. In a precarious situation, the British group hoped to sell Pinault France for a good price. It wanted, in fact, to sell back to François Pinault not only the company that he had created but more significantly, its subsidiary, Luterma. This wasn't a solution that interested the entrepreneur. The final act in their tussle happened on the night of November 29, 1974. For almost two weeks, Jean Leprince, Jean-Rémy Jacquemin, and Hubert Guidal had been at the Luterma headquarters in La Courneuve negotiating with the British. When François Pinault arrived on the 29th, a Friday, he wanted it over with. The discussions intensified and continued relentlessly late into the night. At three o'clock in the morning, of what was by now November 30, an agreement was finally signed. François Pinault bought his company for 10 million francs, 15 million less than what the British had paid for it. Once again "commando mode" proved its effectiveness.

For all that, though, it takes audacity to buy back your company when the market in which it operates is at a standstill, awash with unsold stock and with dramatically reduced revenue. François Pinault was taking a big risk. The danger was even greater because the supply contracts that Pinault France signed before the crisis were established when wood prices were high. Since those had fallen through, the company owed some 50 million francs, a considerable sum that put the company at risk of outright bankruptcy. But François Pinault quickly found a solution. "His strategy was to keep the purchase of Pinault France secret for four days. Suppliers

were convinced that both Luterma and Pinault France were about to file for bankruptcy. They scrambled to collect their goods or secure certified checks. François Pinault took advantage of this panic to dissolve the old contracts," Hubert Guidal later told Jean Bothorel. Convinced they were on the verge of losing everything, suppliers preferred to recuperate their goods or to waive delivery for those Pinault France had ordered, with the company taking charge of the cancellation fees. In the end, the company had to pay suppliers "just" 10 million francs in arrears. Some found fault with the maneuver, but such criticism does not diminish this testament to François Pinault's business acumen. In unsuccessfully renegotiating their contracts, a number of competitors found themselves in critical financial situations and were forced to permanently close their doors.

By the beginning of December 1974, François Pinault had dealt with the most pressing matters. But his company's situation was far from guaranteed. It would take almost two years before it would begin to recover. Two years during which the entrepreneur dramatically reduced costs, cut his employees' salaries, with their consent—he refused, however, to lay anyone off—and did not shy away from selling his timber stock at a loss. This was unheard of in the industry, but it gave the company what it most needed: cash to buy new wood at a good price and thus relaunch the import and distribution cycle. Above all, François Pinault decided to expand his horizons, looking beyond Scandinavia for his wood; this time he had his sights set on Canada. But the approach had to be carefully considered: the supply chain was simplified in order to reduce costs. Wood exports from North America traditionally traveled via the West Coast, which meant going through the Panama Canal. For François Pinault, this took too long, and more importantly, it was too expensive. His plan was to export wood from the East Coast directly to Saint-Malo. Preparations took some time. In 1975, Hubert Guidal was sent to Quebec to evaluate the situation. In November, François Pinault traveled to Canada to sign an initial contract for 39,240 cubic yards (30,000 cubic meters) of wood per year. While there, he established invaluable relations with the American businessman John Ryan, who was to be in charge of organizing deliveries to France. For this purpose, François Pinault created his own shipping company: Agence Maritime de Bretagne. That way, he controlled the transport of his timber. This was groundbreaking in the industry and another step in eliminating middlemen.

Gambling on Canadian timber was a bold, even risky, move. While the new supply chain enabled a 20 percent reduction in the price of timber from Canada, there were a number of uncertainties, starting with shipping in the North Atlantic, a zone subject to strong currents and frequent storms. In addition, François Pinault did not know the actual capacity of Quebec wood producers and if ongoing long-term deliveries would be possible. He ultimately signed the first contract without a trial run. Who could say if the operation would go smoothly? In the end, the fears all proved unfounded, and the gamble paid off. By the first half of the 1980s, Pinault France was responsible for one-third of all France's timber imports.

In establishing a new supply route, the entrepreneur had, once again, revolutionized industry practices, which had long been loyal to the Scandinavian supply system. Amid a crisis, he focused on innovation and expansion, rejecting the defensive strategy taken by his competitors. Finally, he gave his company an international dimension, prefigured by his first trips to Sweden and Finland in 1965. The entrepreneur was now aware of what he had to gain by seizing opportunities elsewhere, even very far from France. This international tropism would come to characterize the company, and it still does today. In 1976, two years after its founder took it over, Pinault France was back on the path to growth. That year, its revenue was 523 million francs and it had 262 employees. It was now ready for a new phase in its development.

Pages 38-39: The Pinault truck fleet at the port of Saint-Malo in the 1970s.
Above: Transporting timber in Canada.

CONSOLIDATING LEADERSHIP (1978-90)

In 1978, Pinault France acquired several of its competitors. Many others would follow. This was a major strategic shift, again breaking with the business world's prevailing practices: François Pinault chose to seize opportunities offered by the crisis to accelerate his growth. This would set the destiny of his company—and his own—on a unique path.

A change of dimension

At the end of the 1970s, the wood industry was facing a critical situation. The collapse of the construction market—between 1975 and 1985, its share of the country's GDP fell by 11 percent—plunged the sector into recession. Every company operating in the sector was affected: importers struggled with soaring costs for freight and transport; trading companies were crippled by the size of their inventories; and sawmills were crushed by energy costs, with their number dropping from 15,000 to 5,000 between 1960 and 1980, while, at the other end of the chain, the order books of timber manufacturers, of parquet floors, doors, and windows, were almost empty. Already critical, the industry's situation worsened with the second oil crisis, which resulted in a fresh surge in oil prices. In the space of a few weeks, the price per barrel went from 13 to 35 US dollars. In 1980, it reached 40 US dollars. The explosion in production costs hit the industry hard. This is clear in the number of companies that failed each year: before 1973, in the timber industry, the annual number was less than 200; this increased to 419 in 1975, 544 in 1978, and 683 in 1981. Among the most striking collapses was that of Sogebois, which shut its doors in 1977.

Within the declining industry, Pinault France stood tall, its prosperity undeniable. Like all its competitors, the company had been affected by the construction market's collapse. However, the new supply route that it had established from Canada, the control of its own shipping, and the sale of its timber stocks had given it a much better pricing structure than other players in the industry. In addition, thanks to its network of agencies, Pinault France was located close to most of its clients, so deliveries could be carried out at a relatively low cost. Controlling the cost of operations both upstream and downstream: the result of a bold and successful strategy initiated in 1965, an approach that enabled the company to maintain a high level of activity and to continue making money. So why not take advantage of it to go even farther?

As early as 1978, François Pinault had decided on his course of action. The time had come for Pinault France to take a new step. Not as it had done in the past, by opening new agencies or industrial centers—by favoring organic growth—but by acquiring companies already established in the market, that is, by decisively focusing on external growth. This strategy enabled it to rapidly gain market share. The time was right: because of the crisis, many of these companies were in a difficult situation, even verging on bankruptcy. They could thus be acquired on favorable terms. In addition, as a measure to avoid social disaster, the state had decided—through the intermediary of the Interministerial Committee for Improving Industrial Structures (CIASI)—to provide subsidies to those taking over liquidated companies and to guarantee the loans necessary to relaunch operations. Pinault France was clearly entitled to this support, which proportionally reduced its financial commitments. François Pinault would later be

43

reproached for buying out his struggling competitors with the aid of public funds. However, in addition to this strategy being supported, even encouraged, by the public authorities, taking over companies facing insurmountable difficulties avoided "social chaos" that would no doubt have been far more significant if bankruptcy proceedings had been taken to their conclusion. Through the acquisition of several competitors, François Pinault kickstarted the timber industry's consolidation. This shift had hardly touched the sector but was already well underway elsewhere—including with food and capital goods—and moving even faster with the crisis.

Thus in 1978, with all the resources available, Pinault France embarked on its first external growth operations. Among the companies acquired were many small trading and import businesses located on the Atlantic coast, where Pinault France was ideally placed to supply retailers and manufacturers. It also acquired larger businesses, such as Duchesne in Honfleur, Dubosc in Bordeaux, and Verry and Mayeux in Saint-Malo. Between 1978 and the early 1980s, François Pinault acquired at least sixty companies, not only in the west of France, but throughout the country. The timber entrepreneur became a corporate investor, a profession that demanded responsiveness, rigor, an ability to rapidly grasp opportunities, and enormous pragmatism. All things at which François Pinault excels.

In certain circles, and particularly in the timber industry, its reputation was not improving. While large groups often took over bankrupt businesses, the practice was much rarer for SMEs, especially in Brittany. It was not customary to profit from the misfortune of others. Even more so because, generally, everyone knew everyone else. "It was perceived poorly, but I didn't care about what people would say," the entrepreneur admitted to Jean Bothorel. By the end of the 1970s, the "Pinault method" was well established. François Pinault relied on a small team, made up of Jean Leprince, Hubert Guidal, Jean-Pierre Andrevon, Jean-Rémy Jacquemin, and Gilles Silberman, a corporate lawyer. "We usually visited the company in difficulty during the day. We would leave in Mr. Pinault's Beechcraft plane and he would carry four apples for lunch. He would carefully inspect the premises while Jacquemin would examine the accounts, and I would check the state of the buildings, the equipment, and the stock. In the evening, we would give our reports to Jean Leprince who would summarize everything. He was then the one who negotiated the takeover with the trustee or the commercial court. The efficiency was diabolical," Hubert Guidal would later tell Jean Bothorel. This "commando" approach made it possible to carry out one acquisition after another at a steady pace. In the early 1980s, Pinault France became France's leading timber importer. In 1980, its revenue reached 1 billion francs and its employees surpassed 1,500. What a journey! In the space of just three years, the company had completely shifted scale. It had left its regional context behind and taken on a genuinely national dimension. Its only real competitors in France were merchants in the Vosges and Jura.

It was at this time that something happened to heighten the concerns of the timber industry's stakeholders and to weaken their situation just a little more: the election of François Mitterrand as President of France on the 10th of May 1981. It is hardly an overstatement to say that the business community was frightened by the new president, a socialist with communist ties. And in fact, the new government's first measures did nothing to reassure them. For example, entire sectors of the economy were nationalized, retirement was reduced to the age of sixty, a fifth week of paid vacation was instituted, as was a thirty-nine-hour work week, and the minimum wage was increased by 10 percent. Those measures resulted in a sharp rise in the cost of labor and a marked jump in unemployment which, in 1981, had already reached 7 percent of the active population. In Rennes, however, François Pinault was not worried by the transition. "I wasn't happy, but I wasn't worried either. Having worked with men from the left, I knew they were people who thought things through. On the morning of Monday, May 11, 1981, I arrived at the office where I found all the employees with long faces. I told them: 'Remember! They will give up. Now is the time to accelerate,'" he recounts in the book by Pierre Daix. The entrepreneur was so unconcerned that, the same day, he visited the BMW dealer in Rennes to buy the carmaker's most elegant model. Once again, François Pinault was going against the grain of the business world. Overall, the latter was transfixed by the left-wing government's arrival, putting all their projects on the back burner; François Pinault, on the other hand, believed that it was the right time to move forward. Did he realize that reality would catch up with the new government and that, in a context of crisis and very high inflation, it would sooner or later seek to reconnect with the business community? It's possible. And that's exactly what happened. In 1983, austerity policies marked the rallying of the left to the market economy. That same year, the Second Marché was created on the Paris Stock Exchange, enabling medium-sized companies to source financing. Twelve months later, the financial and stock markets were liberalized.

Far from being interrupted, François Pinault's external growth strategy, initiated in 1978, accelerated from 1981. This was aided by the state's continued subsidies for those taking over companies in difficulty. The Breton entrepreneur was among those accessing such support. In the 1980s, he stepped up acquisitions, not only in timber trading and importing, but also, and more importantly, in industry, including taking over manufacturers of parquet floors, doors, windows, and sofas (Guermonprez, Jean Prévost), and kitchen furnishings for private and public facilities (Lafa-Ranger). Having focused on the industry's upstream, interest was now in the downstream. Among many acquisitions, there was one of particular importance: Isoroy. Founded via a government initiative in 1982, it was the result of the merger of a trio of wood panel companies: Isorel, Leroy, and Baradel, all three in serious difficulty. Employing 4,300 people, it had eleven plants with revenue of 2 billion francs. In short, an industrial giant, but a fragile one! It was to avoid the three companies going bankrupt that the state had instituted the group. But this "industrial conglomeration" didn't solve anything. In 1984, having exhausted 675 million francs in aid, Isoroy was on the verge of collapse. It was then, in 1986, that François Pinault became interested.

In doing so, he was taking on considerable risk. Isoroy was a company in the midst of collapse, one that had never really found its place in the market and it could drag Pinault France to the bottom of the abyss. Jean-Paul Amiel, Managing Director of Crédit Lyonnais—Pinault France's bank but also one of the major shareholders in Isoroy—was stunned when the Breton entrepreneur told him of his plan to make an offer. He warned him, "Isoroy is overextended and very deep in the red." For François Pinault, the operation held a dual interest: it would enable him to double in size and, above all, to become the European leader in timber. In the spring of 1986, François Pinault decided to take the chance: he presented his offer to the Interministerial Committee on Industrial Restructuring (CIRI), the organization that had succeeded the CIASI in 1982. The entrepreneur was straightforward in laying out his conditions: takeover in fifteen days, purchase of all stock for a symbolic price of 1 franc and of accounts receivable at a preferential rate, as well as a payment of 600 million francs in public aid, all in exchange for retaining the 3,600 employees. After hesitating and encouraging an alternative proposition—the ministries considered him more a trader than an industrialist—the public authorities ultimately accepted his offer. His major asset was his commitment to not dismantling the business. François Pinault also benefited from the crucial support of the president of the Commercial Court of Caen, who was impressed by his success with earlier takeovers. He would have to make do, however, with 250 million francs in public aid. In all, it would take François Pinault and his team less than a year to turn Isoroy around. In the beginning, the entrepreneur had a reputation as a fierce buyer, and he committed his own capital to the project while facing opposition from some staff and local elected officials. He also aroused the concern of the company's creditors. But he did not allow himself to be intimidated: determined to restabilize a company that would bring a new dimension to his group, he resolutely set about its recovery: one factory was closed and the workforce was reduced from 4,300 to 3,300, while the management team was streamlined to some twenty executives. Production facilities were modernized, computerization picked up pace, and the "Pinault France culture" was introduced, ensuring that the company was more flexible, lighter, and more reactive. As a result, in 1987, the group made a profit of 100 million francs, the first since its creation in 1982. "It was with Isoroy that our scale really changed," François Pinault explained to his biographer, Pierre Daix. The deal was a major part of the group's expansion into manufacturing. We will return to the portrait of Pinault France at the end of the 1980s. For the moment, the experience acquired in taking over Isoroy constituted an invaluable asset for completing another major external growth operation: the takeover of the paper group Chapelle Darblay.

A new challenge

With more than 2,000 employees, revenue of around 1.2 billion francs, and two factories, in Saint-Étienne-du-Rouvray and Grand-Couronne, Chapelle Darblay occupied a unique place in the French industrial landscape. Created in 1968 from the merging of Darblay and the Papeteries de la Chapelle paper mills, this paper industry giant produced 40 percent of France's paper, including 85 percent of its newsprint, an indication of its highly strategic position. But the group had been struggling with insurmountable difficulties since the late 1970s. As was the case with many other companies, it was hard hit by the oil crises of 1973 and 1979. Its productivity was mediocre and its workforce bloated. The cost-cutting measures that had been put in place were not enough. In 1984, public authorities finally decided to hand the reins of Chapelle Darblay to the Canadian businessman John Kila, who had just completed the restructuring of the Dutch paper group Parenco. Appointed CEO, he was assigned 3.3 billion francs in state support. End of act one.

The second act opened in 1986. That year, as the group's situation continued to deteriorate and anomalies were noticed in John Kila's management, the public authorities decided to put an end to state financing,

L'EMPIRE PINAULT
SE RASSEMBLE

Le groupe lève le voile sur sa nouvelle organisation : 117 entreprises
industrielles classées en sept divisions. Un fil conducteur : la filière bois

Avec 7,5 à 7,8 milliards de francs de chiffre d'affaires dont 10 % à l'exportation, plus de 300 millions de francs de profits prévus cette année, un effectif dépassant les 10 000 personnes, 140 points de vente dans le négoce, 43 usines de panneaux, menuiseries, parquets, lambris, maisons à ossature bois, meubles... Pinault lance une vaste offensive sur le marché de la construction et du cadre de vie. Et projette, si les vents sont favorables, une introduction en Bourse à l'automne prochain.

Pinault sort de l'ombre... Le groupe attaque sur tous les fronts de la filière bois avec des outils de production modernisés, rentabilisés, un réseau de distribution bien structuré, renforcé, partout où la conjoncture du bâtiment semble en pointe, et une équipe de jeunes managers (la moyenne d'âge est de 40 ans), des «patrons de choc» rompus aux techniques modernes du commerce, de la production industrielle, de la gestion...

François Pinault, qui vient de quitter sa panoplie de «repreneur masqué» d'entreprises pour forger l'image de marque, la politique de communication du groupe et planter bien haut l'étendard Pinault, a connu un premier succès : la constitution d'un empire dans la filière bois, à la fois de production et de distribution. Pour cela, il lui aura fallu rassembler

en une quinzaine d'années toutes les entités nécessaires par des rachats successifs de sociétés, des créations, des extensions d'unités industrielles... plaçant et dosant les ingrédients au bon moment pour amener ces affaires sur les chemins de la croissance et de la rentabilité. Le tout le plus possible par autofinancement, affirme-t-il.

DIVERSIFICATION DANS LE BOIS. Pour ce négociant de talent, as de la finance, qui a débuté dans le commerce des bois à Rennes en 1963, le trésor de guerre amassé, dans les années 70, grâce, dit-on, au placement habile du produit de la vente en 1973 de la majorité du capital de la société Pinault (qu'il rachètera en 1975...) à un groupe britannique, a constitué un puissant levier.

Ayant repris la barre de l'entreprise, F. Pinault a développé ensuite une double stratégie de diversification dans tous les métiers du bois, tout en

étendant le réseau des centres de distribution. Dans la foulée, il a pris pied dans l'affrètement maritime, le transport aérien, l'achat et la gestion de matériels, le bricolage (avec Bricofrance en 1979), le négoce du bâtiment, l'aménagement et la rénovation de la maison... Des prolongements logiques.

Un développement spectaculaire ensuite puisque entre 1982 et 1986 le chiffre d'affaires du groupe Pinault est passé de 1,8 à 7 milliards de francs. La reprise d'Isoroy en 1986 pèse lourd dans la balance : plus d'un milliard et demi de francs de chiffre d'affaires. Le monde des affaires a découvert à cette occasion le «Tapie» de la filière bois que la reprise de La Chapelle-d'Arblay avec la société papetière québécoise Cascades, a poussé plus encore sur le devant de la scène. Mais les structures du groupe restant encore floues, F. Pinault, désireux d'accéder à de nouvelles sources de financement par une in-

LE MONITEUR/29 JANVIER 198

Left: An article in *Le Moniteur* in 1988.
Right: François Pinault in the daily newspaper *Ouest-France* in 1987.

further weakening the company's position. It was at that point that François Pinault chose to step forward. He had been watching the paper group's evolution for some time, and the more it plunged into crisis, the more the Breton entrepreneur regarded it as a candidate for acquisition. The idea was not as radical as it may seem at first glance because producing paper requires wood, and Chapelle Darblay consumed around one million steres per year. Through its acquisition, François Pinault would strengthen his position downstream in the timber industry and gain access to an advanced industrial facility. François Pinault had once again shown an astonishing ability to seize opportunities when they appeared, even if it meant taking considerable risks. And there were risks. François Pinault may have proven himself as a buyer of companies, but Chapelle Darblay was a much bigger operation than Isoroy, and while they had things in common, paper pulp and timber are two very different businesses. Most importantly, the state had warned that the buyer would not receive any subsidies. But it would take much more than that to discourage François Pinault. So when John Kila resigned on October 30, 1987, François Pinault requested an urgent loan of 250 billion francs from Crédit Lyonnais—which was approved—before presenting to the commercial court the offer he had put together with the Canadian group Cascades. It was accepted on November 2, 1987. After a few legal wrangles, the sale to the two partners was completed for 300 million francs. François Pinault acted personally to close the deal, rather than in the name of his company, thus protecting Pinault France if things did not go well. Crédit Lyonnais also took a 15 percent stake in the paper giant.

The next stage of the adventure would prove more difficult. Once again, François Pinault and his team set themselves apart with their reactivity. As early as November, they acquired, at a good price, an enormous quantity of coniferous trees, among the thousands felled by the storm that hit France on October 17, 1987. These would supply the Saint-Étienne-du-Rouvray factory. The timber freight operated by the national rail network, the SNCF, was also optimized to reduce costs. François Pinault, like John Kila before him, could not avoid reducing the group's workforce. The measure, though, triggered a strike that lasted several days; it even found him sequestered inside his office, which did not stop him from leading the negotiations with the unions himself. That undertaking avoided the risk of other social conflicts. One year after the takeover, Chapelle Darblay was still far from stable, but revenue had started to increase. François Pinault had also bought shares in Cascades and had personally invested 300 million francs in capital. He now held 85 percent of the company, with 15 percent remaining at Crédit Lyonnais. In spring 1989, as the recovery was continuing, the Breton entrepreneur sold his shares at cost to Pinault France for 450 million francs.

A group active across the industry

By the end of the 1980s, Pinault France had become a major player in French industry. With revenue in excess of 10 billion francs (including Chapelle Darblay) and more than 8,000 employees, the group did not yet appear in the top 100 French companies that the press had begun publishing annually. But it dominated the French timber industry and had established itself as a European leader. Its most striking feature was its positioning across the

A Pinault truck being loaded at Saint-Malo in the 1980s.

entire industry, "from the forest to the dining room," as the founder summed it up. François Pinault himself had become a prominent figure in business circles. In 1983, at the invitation of Ambroise Roux, the all-powerful "godfather of French capitalism" as he was sometimes called, he joined the French Association of Private Enterprises (AFEP). Created in 1982 in reaction to the economic policy implemented by the left-wing government, it brought together the elite of French industrialists. "When Ambroise Roux called to ask me to join, I thought it was a joke at first. But his tone was unequivocal. I went to see him in Paris. He wanted to transform the AFEP's membership," François Pinault told Pierre Daix. A wonderful tribute to his career. On Rue La Boétie in Paris, where the association was headquartered, the Breton entrepreneur could now rub shoulders with such illustrious industrialists and financiers as Jean-Marc Vernes (Béghin Say), Guy Dejouany (Générale des Eaux), Jean-Paul Parayre (Dumez), and Jacques Calvet (PSA).

In the late 1980s, in parallel to making a number of acquisitions, the entrepreneur carried out a major reorganization of his group's structure. The group then had three main divisions: Pinault-Distribution, which includes the historical activities of importing and trading timber; France-Bois Industries (carpentry, parquet, and paneling); and the Compagnie Internationale d'Ameublement (kitchen and office furniture). In turn, these three entities controlled a cascade of companies. Despite its size, the group continued to be managed in a very flexible way, as it had been for a decade. To run his projects, François Pinault continued to rely on a handful of collaborators, guaranteeing rapid decisions and execution, one of the cornerstones of the company's success. Over the years, however, the small team that not so long ago had been traveling around France with François Pinault, experienced some changes. Some had left, including Jean Leprince, Gilles Silberman, and Jean-Pierre Andrevon; others remained, such as Hubert Guidal. Newcomers had joined the group, such as Jean-Paul Amiel, who came from Crédit Lyonnais, Patricia Barbizet, the former Financial Director at Renault Crédit International, who came on board as Financial Director in 1989, and Hervé Guillaume, the former Sales Director with Renault Véhicules Industriels, who was appointed head of Isoroy. Among these recent arrivals was François Pinault's eldest son, François-Henri. "The company was part of my world: my father talked about it a lot. I was, however, completely free to choose the focus of my studies. I wasn't under any pressure to join the group, but in doing so, I was offered prospects I couldn't hope for elsewhere," he says today.

Born in 1962, and a graduate of HEC Paris, François-Henri Pinault joined the company in 1987. He and his father immediately came to an agreement. "We decided that I should not report to him and that he should not be my direct boss. And in fact, that didn't happen until 2001," he explains. Like many of his colleagues, he started on the ground floor. "I started with an integration internship. I found myself in a sawmill for exotic wood in Honfleur. Then I was a salesman in a warehouse in Évreux, after which I joined Pinault-Distribution, where I was in charge of establishing a central purchasing office," he recalls. In 1988, he became head of France-Bois Industries, where he quickly had to implement major restructuring. "That's when I really came to grips with the group's culture, which can be summarized by the phrase 'Those are helped who help themselves.' We couldn't just continue with business as usual. We had to constantly act and find solutions. It was sometimes very difficult. But it was also very educational," he continues. In 1991, with a more than honorable record, François-Henri was named head of Pinault-Distribution. A new challenge for the twenty-nine-year-old. The team—made up of seasoned professionals from large groups and a few younger employees—working alongside François Pinault contributed to the group's professionalization. Their arrival and the ensuing transformations to its organization also reduced the managerial focus on François Pinault, which had been the group's defining characteristic since its creation. This was an important change at a time when the group was experiencing constant growth.

The company took a decisive step forward on October 25, 1988: it was listed on the Second Marché of the Paris Stock Exchange as Pinault SA. With a listed value of 856.5 million francs, François Pinault now held 50 percent of the company's capital. For the group, this was a major change: it faced new legal obligations and it had to learn to communicate with shareholders and take care of its image. By going public, Pinault SA had given itself the means to raise new capital to finance its planned developments. One of these was particularly important because of the consequences it would have for the group's future: the takeover of the Compagnie Française de l'Afrique Occidentale (CFAO).

CFAO: Moving into specialized distribution

March 1989: Serge Weinberg visited François Pinault in his offices on Avenue Marceau. The former Chief of Staff to Laurent Fabius when the latter was Minister of the Budget (1981-82), he had become Managing Director of Pallas Finance, the mergers and acquisitions consulting subsidiary of Banque Pallas. They met to discuss something that interested François Pinault: the Compagnie Française d'Afrique Occidentale (CFAO). Behind that name, which dates to the colonial era—was a company created in 1852 to trade cocoa, peanuts, and rubber. Present in electrical distribution (with Compagnie de Distribution de Matériel Électrique – CDME), food distribution (with the supermarket chain Ruche Méridionale), automobile, bicycle, and equipment distribution, including construction equipment, transport, and retail, it was a highly diversified conglomerate with revenue of 32 billion francs, but with a precarious financial situation. The company's head, Pierre Paoli, had gradually withdrawn from the African continent—which in 1989 represented only 15 percent of its activity compared to 51 percent in 1983—and had expanded his sometimes questionable investments in French and foreign companies. This strategy worried CFAO's main shareholders, the Swiss holding company Pargesa, the shipping company Delmas-Vieljeux, the insurance firm UAP, and the bank Crédit Lyonnais. In this context, the entry of a new shareholder could facilitate the company's strategic reorientation and thus reassure the existing investors. This was why Serge Weinberg had sought a meeting with François Pinault.

The latter was immediately interested. For some time, the entrepreneur had believed that the model on which his success was based—concentration on a single sector, the timber industry, and its extension, that of paper—needed to be thoroughly rethought. This conviction was based on one observation: in both the timber and paper industries, competition was becoming increasingly aggressive, whether from the United States, Northern Europe, Asia, or even, more recently, Eastern Europe. Since USSR president Mikhail Gorbachev launched perestroika in 1985—the vast

Wooden planks stored at Saint-Malo in the 1980s.

program of economic and social reforms—the countries of Eastern Europe, once under the Soviet Union's yoke, had gradually become part of world trade. This phenomenon would increase dramatically after the fall of the Berlin Wall in November 1989. These countries, like those in Asia, had a double competitive advantage: abundant resources and low production costs. To maintain or expand their positions, these large European and American groups had intensified their investments, taking over smaller competitors or building large, ultra-modern plants. In France's paper sector in 1989 alone, the Finnish group United Paper Mills launched construction of a large factory in Alsace, while its Norwegian counterpart Norske Skogindustrier began work on a new site at Golbey in the Vosges and the American company International Paper was preparing to take over the Aussedat-Rey paper mills in the Haute-Vienne department.

For François Pinault, there was absolutely no doubt: in the timber industry, as in the paper industry, it would be increasingly difficult to resist competition from new manufacturing countries and from large industrial groups. The only chance was a significant investment: to be able to compete with United Paper Mills or International Paper would require an injection of at least 4 billion francs into the two factories operated by Chapelle Darblay in Saint-Étienne du Rouvray and Grand-Couronne. That was a considerable sum, and there was no guarantee that it would be enough, nor that the investment would create profitability. There was one other decisive factor that François Pinault was undoubtedly one of the first to perceive: in industry, constraints connected to environmental protection would become increasingly more important. These would further increase production costs. For all these reasons—the impact of European competition, the opening up of Eastern Europe, the accelerated development of Asian markets, and environmental regulations—the Pinault group would sooner or later have to withdraw from the timber and paper industries and concentrate on new activities. After beginning its shift from a trading company to professional distribution in timber and building materials in the 1970s and 1980s, François Pinault was now considering specialized distribution. "When I visited the United States and Canada, I could see that future developments would focus on the consumer. So I had the idea of shifting my activities toward distribution," he explains in Pierre Daix's book. "He saw that the economy was evolving—to a certain extent at the expense of the manufacturers—and that it was thus necessary to rely on distribution companies. From there, a series of opportunities arose," according to Patricia Barbizet.[3]

CFAO offered the first of these opportunities. Within this group, François Pinault was particularly interested in one activity: electrical distribution organized within CDME. This business had revenue of 10 billion francs. It also served the same client base as Pinault SA: construction and renovation professionals. The synergies were clear. Thanks to CFAO, the Breton group could begin its move toward distribution. But there was another reason for François Pinault's interest: CFAO would greatly enhance Pinault SA's international dimension. First, it would give it a foothold in the African continent, which still represented a major part of the company's activities. François Pinault was one of the few in France who believed in Africa. For some time, French entrepreneurs had been leaving the African continent in droves, investing instead in Eastern Europe, seen as the new El Dorado. The cautious Breton entrepreneur believed that, for once, it was better to wait before following the current. Especially as the French risked encountering German competitors on the ground. By avoiding Eastern

3   In Pierre Daix's book.

Europe for the moment and continuing to concentrate on Africa, François Pinault was clearly going against his peers. But it went beyond Africa: CFAO was also active in the United States and in a large part of Western Europe, which represented 60 percent of its revenue. Thus, the company would dramatically broaden Pinault SA's geographical horizons. This had been an integral component of its development since the Scandinavian adventure in 1965.

In the early summer of 1989, François Pinault gave Serge Weinberg and Banque Pallas a mandate to purchase as many CFAO shares on the stock market as possible. His idea was, of course, to eventually take control of the company. In December of that year, he already held 20.5 percent of its capital, making him the company's largest shareholder. By the beginning of 1990, his stake had risen to more than 33 percent. What followed was no surprise: in March 1990, Paul Paoli handed his position as CEO of CFAO to François Pinault. With the agreement of the other shareholders, he immediately began to reorient the group's activities: thus, Ruche Méridionale, its administrative and transport activities, as well as the distribution of bicycles and selected retail subsidiaries—notably in the United States and Australia—were sold. CFAO refocused on specialized distribution (particularly of electrical equipment and automobiles), services and trade, with a strong presence in Europe and Africa.

The takeover was going ahead at full speed, in parallel with the sale of Chapelle Darblay. The entry into specialized distribution and the exit from the paper industry were two sides of the same strategy. On April 2, 1990, Pinault SA sold the paper group it had acquired in 1987 to Finland's Kymmene for 1.32 billion francs. Chapelle Darblay's recovery since its takeover was obvious. A part of the sale's proceeds was returned to the state as repayment for advances made during the takeover. With this operation, François Pinault began his exit from the timber industry. Advancing gradually, it would take several years to complete.

A crucial new step happened on September 24, 1990. That was the day that Pinault SA absorbed CFAO. The small company—with revenue of 10 billion francs—swallowed the larger company, whose revenue, after divestments, exceeded 20 billion francs. The operation resulted in a group with 30,000 employees, and a presence in thirty-one countries. Barely three decades after its creation, the company François Pinault had founded passed a milestone. It was not the only company to expand its horizons and shift scale. The fall of the Berlin Wall kickstarted globalization, leading to a vast restructuring of French capitalism. The focus everywhere was on external growth, the conquest of new markets, and the diversification of activities, all necessary to take advantage of the opportunities offered by the opening of borders, or to reach critical mass in the face of competition. A few examples: in 1990, Bouygues and the Compagnie Générale des Eaux began exploring the Russian market and BSN rapidly diversified into the baked goods industry, while Lyonnaise des Eaux merged with Dumez, number two in French construction and public works companies. The following year, in 1991, Bolloré took control of the shipping company Delmas-Vieljeux. Pinault SA was not the only one to announce its ambitions loud and clear. It was, however, rethinking its model. It was not merely a question of growing or diversifying, but of totally reinventing itself. In fact, with the takeover of CFAO, a new group was about to launch.

Left: François Pinault in the magazine *L'Expansion* in 1987.
Right: François Pinault with former President Jacques Chirac at Versailles in 2008.
The two men first met in 1972, during the acquisition of a carpentry workshop in Meymac,
in the Corrèze region. Their friendship spanned several decades.

A WORD FROM OUR FRIENDS

A WORD
FROM
OUR
FRIENDS

Jean-Jacques Aillagon

François Pinault quickly established himself as a leading figure in our country's cultural landscape, as early as the 1990s. His reputation as a mindful, passionate collector of contemporary art was firmly established. So it came as no surprise when he announced, in 2000, his project to open a museum to show his collection. At the time, I was president of the Centre Pompidou and was well aware of just how much such an initiative could consolidate but also enhance the influence of Paris. Little did I know that a few years later, I would get to be part of this great cultural adventure. While the museum planned for Boulogne-Billancourt never did come to fruition, for reasons that are well known, in the years that followed other museums embodied François Pinault's vision: in Venice, at the Palazzo Grassi and Punta della Dogana, and in Paris with the Bourse de Commerce. I realized that François Pinault's cultural endeavor was exceptional and unique because it was driven by a passion for art and artists; it had become his lifeblood, essential to his life. This passion was underpinned by a rare quality, one that cannot be replaced by any intellect or scholarship:

intuition. The intuition that an artwork can resist the test of time and fashions, the intuition that an artist has something to say, the intuition that a place is made for art, the intuition that an architect—often Tadao Ando—is the right person for the job. There is a reason that François Pinault's cultural adventure was made with enlightened and loyal companions. It is his trademark. It is what sets him apart, as does the decision to house each of his museums in landmark historic buildings, as if to assert that the dialogue between heritage and creation is necessary and dynamic, and to highlight the absurdity of opposing them. François Pinault wanted to share this passion, these convictions, with the public by opening up his collection. He also wanted them to be the foundation of not only his commitment but that of his entire family, especially François-Henri Pinault, who has been involved in all of his initiatives, each of his projects, each of his dreams.

Jean-Jacques Aillagon, former French Minister of Culture

Carlo Capasa

François-Henri Pinault and I met in 2006, during a Rolling Stones concert in Los Angeles. We'd both been invited by Mick Jagger, and we spent an unforgettable day together, which ended with the concert. When it was over, François-Henri and I were both much more exhausted than Mick, who was bursting with energy.

We share a passion for music, but that isn't the only thing. We are both passionate about fashion, excellence, the Made in Italy legacy, sustainability, and more than anything else, people: these are central to our always fascinating discussions. François-Henri is a champion of responsible business, protecting the environment and people.

This dedication led to his being presented with the GCFA Visionary Award in 2019, at our annual fashion sustainability awards. The award recognizes his focus on putting the issue at the center of his business strategy, and for creating, along with the French government, the Fashion Pact initiative, a coalition for sustainable fashion.

The Kering group that he chairs has also placed a strong emphasis on gender equality, and demonstrated its commitment, as evidenced by the research for Supporting Women in the Luxury Supply Chain, undertaken by Kering and presented in 2021 at "Including Diversity," an event organized by the National Chamber for Italian Fashion to promote diversity, equity, and inclusion in the fashion industry.

As president of the National Chamber for Italian Fashion, I would like to thank François-Henri Pinault for his invaluable work at Kering. For his initiatives, projects, and vision, and for his recognition of Italian creativity and expertise, for the way he has valued and promoted the Italian brands that are part of his group and, in turn, Made in Italy. I personally thank him for the example he sets and for how positive making his acquaintance has been for me.

Carlo Capasa, President, Camera Nazionale della Moda Italiana (National Chamber for Italian Fashion)

Jean-Michel Darrois

For a lawyer, being part of the emergence, rise, and transformation of an independently-owned company into a global group in less than twenty years is an exceptional opportunity.

In 1989, François Pinault "came out of the woodwork," leaving a sector he considered threatened by foreign competition to venture into specialized distribution and retail, a sector that he saw as highly promising, and to take on the stock market, at the time still unfamiliar to him. For a man with no experience of Paris's business and commercial world, it was a risky double gambit. But following the advice of a young banker, Serge Weinberg, he took the risk and succeeded, taking control, despite strong opposition, of CFAO, a listed company more than a century old, specializing in the distribution of a range of products, from cars to medicines, mainly in Africa.

From that time on, the Pinault group, now listed on the stock exchange, expanded through a series of divestments and acquisitions. The boss left his staff and advisers little time to rest.

Just before an Easter weekend, they were summoned urgently to negotiate night and day—which is the norm now, but at the time was not at all—the sale of Ruche Méridionale to Casino.

In the early hours of the morning, Mr. Guichard, convinced by François Pinault, agreed to place a very large check, drawn against his personal account, into escrow.

The major shift to distribution and retail had already taken place. Several groups were interested in buying the Maus-Nordmann family's stake in Printemps but were reluctant to take on the legal risks the deal involved. According to the prevailing law, if the acquisition of the shares gave their acquirer more than 50 percent of the voting rights, the latter was then obliged to file a takeover bid for all the company's shares. This obligation was limited to 66 percent if the acquired voting rights did not confer 50 percent control. On the afternoon of November 22, 1991, the Pinault group outlined a proposition to the owners of Printemps: to buy the holding company that held their shares for 3.3 billion francs, on condition that they were first converted into bearer shares in order to strip them of the double voting rights conferred by the length of time that they had been held. The communication methods were archaic. We waited several hours to sign and pay, before receiving, despite the impatience of François Pinault and his adviser, Alain Minc, confirmation by fax of the transfer of the bearer shares. The deal was unsuccessfully challenged before the stock exchange authorities and the Paris Court of Appeal, which confirmed the deal's validity and endorsed it.

Following that case, the mandatory 66 percent takeover bid was abolished and raised to 100 percent.

Among those bidding for Printemps, only François Pinault had, in a matter of hours, analyzed the risk, agreed to take it on, and convinced Crédit Lyonnais to finance it.

Eight years later, Gucci's bosses, Tom Ford and Domenico De Sole were looking for a "white knight" to help them defend themselves against what they considered an "attack": LVMH's acquisition of 34 percent of its capital. They found their knight in PPR, which agreed to subscribe to a capital increase to raise its stake in Gucci to 42 percent, without a clear picture of the company's situation, while LVMH's stake was reduced to 20.6 percent.

The battle between the two groups, which went before the Dutch courts, kept the media spellbound for a long time, fascinated as it was by the unusual showdown between two major French groups.

Both sides took major legal and media blows. Bankers and lawyers on each side clashed violently, and at the same time took steps to find a settlement. Until the morning of September 11, 2001, all attempts failed: that morning, a settlement was reached, following a night of discussions, disputes, and meetings. The bankers and lawyers were exhausted, their faces wan, their dark circles deep, their shirts damp and creased.

To simplify matters, PPR—which had in the meantime acquired Yves Saint Laurent—would take control of Gucci and LVMH would sell its shares.

The saga came to an end during the night of September 10, 2001. A few hours later in New York, on the morning of September 11, the twin towers of the World Trade Center collapsed. Chaos and terror swept the world.

I immediately called François Pinault: "Sir, it won't be easy, but under the circumstances, we can try and get the contract canceled." Without a moment's hesitation, he replied, "No I never go back on my word."

These few examples may help illustrate some of the qualities that helped create and expand the group.

Above all, an ongoing, independent, and original process of deliberation, one that enabled us to anticipate social and economic developments that are often imperceptible to most competitors and experts. For example, in early 2001 many analysts had a pessimistic outlook for the luxury economy. Everyone knows what followed...

Another quality is the ability to rapidly analyze risks and make decisions just as quickly. And finally, a secret blend of seduction and authority to lead your teams and convince your stakeholders. Few entrepreneurs combine all these abilities. To these, François Pinault adds a concern for others that is rare in the corporate world. Looking at François-Henri Pinault, these qualities clearly run in the family.

Jean-Michel Darrois, lawyer

Mercedes Erra

Ten years of Kering? I'm almost surprised. It seems to me that the group chaired by François-Henri Pinault has been around for much longer. At the time of the name change, I remember thinking how inspired it was to adopt a name pronounced like the beautiful English word *care*. *Caring*: taking care, a visionary word a decade ago, whereas today we talk constantly of companies taking care of their natural, human, and social environments. The meaning held within the name gives a clear direction. It is also apropos for a company born from a family business. What could be more "caring" than a family?

The Pinault family has always seemed free and committed to its vision of a capitalism mindful of its impact on society. It is no surprise that the company was one of the first to make a strong and long-term commitment to women. Its evolution from wood, to materials, and then from distribution and retail to luxury has brought it into direct contact with those who make its fortune: women, all over the world. And if there is one topic that extends across all regions of the world and all social classes, it is violence against women. The influence of Salma Hayek Pinault was undoubtedly decisive since her foundation was also grappling with the issue in Mexico.

Violence against women is not an easy topic for a company—no one wants to hear about it—so it requires a strong will and conviction to take it on, and to initiate and support actions that matter. Among these are the Maison des Femmes in the Paris suburb of Saint-Denis, emblematic of this struggle in France and of what needs to be done to change the situation. The Kering Foundation has woven its web on all continents, with NGOs and local stakeholders, to support survivors, to try to defuse violence at its roots with the younger generation, and to mobilize as many on-the-ground players as possible. Since 2008, thousands of women and children have been helped by the Kering Foundation.

When it comes to deciding where and on what to dedicate energy, time, and money for a cause like this, it is determination that makes the difference. I admire this policy of such a vital and deserving fight. In Salma and François-Henri I see a sincerity and a sense of urgency that are rare.

By caring for women, Kering continues to imbue meaning to its name.

Mercedes Erra, Founding President, BETC Group

Jane Fonda

Some of us who, like me, have entered serious old age, remember nostalgically when corporations and banks behaved ethically, were committed to the communities they served, and there were more unions to protect workers' interests. But alas, even then, women's rights, opportunities, and safety were not even an afterthought.

Unfortunately, with the advent of globalization and the corporate takeover of government in too many countries, people are having to fight against corporations that lie, cheat, pollute, and even kill us, seemingly without compunction, to protect their profits. (I'm thinking particularly of fossil fuel and chemical companies and the banks that finance them.) For these behemoths, the bottom line is all that matters.

Imagine my shock on discovering a major anomaly to this greedy, dangerous corporate trend: the Kering group. Here is a company that cares about its people, specifically its women. It has established programs that have nothing to do with the bottom line but instead are aimed at protecting women employees and helping them rise through the ranks.

68

I am friends with the wonderful actor, director, and producer Salma Hayek. Over the years, she and I have worked together, alongside Eve Ensler (author of *The Vagina Monologues* and founder of V-Day: Until the Violence Stops, and One Billion Rising), to stop violence against women. In 2009, Salma married François-Henri Pinault, Kering's Chairman and CEO, which is how I met him and learned about the group.

I'll never forget it; I was stunned: this powerful man was deeply committed to supporting women in myriad ways. A genuine rarity. Salma and François-Henri talked to me at length about what Kering wanted to do, not only for its own employees—more than half of whom are women—but for all the staff of the many fashion houses it owns. François-Henri told me the group was training staff members to support employees who had experienced domestic violence, helping them access local organizations that specialize in helping survivors. Kering funds such groups and offers specific safety measures to any employee experiencing domestic violence, including changing work hours and location to protect them as well as financial aid. These things reveal an unusual corporate sensitivity.

I learned that Kering has also launched programs that help women attain senior management positions. Additionally, helping all staff, the group offers Baby Leave, which provides fourteen weeks of paid leave for any worker who becomes a parent.

In 2015, Kering brought its caring to the film world and created *Women In Motion*. I was honored with the first Women In Motion Award and am very impressed that this program has expanded its vision to include women technicians in the film industry. Kering clearly understands that women see the world differently than men do, experience things like war, work, bankruptcy, and climate change differently than men do, and that if we do not encourage women directors, writers, and technicians to tell stories from a woman's perspective, we'll only get half the picture.

It's clear to me that Kering is not a "half-the-picture" kind of company. François-Henri Pinault and his team have drilled deep and developed a real understanding of gender violence and gender disparity and how these things damage our world. I was extremely inspired when the Kering group joined with Promundo several years ago to launch the Global Boyhood Initiative in North America, to help young boys embrace healthy masculinity and gender equality.

François-Henri Pinault knows that to blossom and become all they are capable of being, women must feel seen, safe, and cherished. Clearly, he wants the woman he lives with and those he works with to feel this way. Let us hope that this example of enlightened behavior, embodied by the Kering group, will spread to other companies. What a brave new world that would be!

Jane Fonda, actress, author, activist

Franz-Olivier Giesbert

Unless you've ever visited a farm, with its manure pit and toil in the fields, you will never understand François Pinault. Having climbed to the pinnacle of the world's highest peaks, he will always remain the stubborn, "wooden-headed" man from a small family farm in Cour Heuzé: 12 hectares and some dozen cows.

That's where it all began, in the second half of the last century, in Trévérien, in Chateaubriand's Brittany, a land hardened by suffering, where the common adage goes: "Better to carry your cross than drag it along." With a driver's license his only viaticum, François Pinault set off, alone, to conquer the world.

In a France where the "élites" prefer to remain "among themselves," this man is an anomaly. He is all the more unusual because he is proud of his rural past, and remains loyal to his old friends from the days when he rolled his Rs, whom he continues to see on weekends, and whose thoughts on the major issues of the day he continues to quote. François Pinault is a man who never forgets anyone or anything.

What secrets lay behind the rapid building of the empire that his eldest son, François-Henri, has since taken over and expanded? First, as strange as it may seem, his sky-blue eyes. As they read your thoughts, they pierce right through you. He's here and there, in the conversation that he's having with you now and then in the next. He's always one step ahead. He anticipates everything that you haven't yet had time to formulate.

And his passion for excellence isn't the least of his virtues. An aesthete and a trailblazer, he imposed his exactitude everywhere. In his business and his patronage. In his museums, from the Collection Pinault in Paris to the Palazzo Grassi and the Punta della Dogana in Venice, he always demands the best. When I was visiting Paul Rebeyrolle one day, the "red" ogre and brilliant painter of nature, trout, and wild boar, told me that he often saw François Pinault, with whom he had forged a "genuine friendship": "When he comes to buy a painting from me, he always takes the right one. Always. He has a good eye."

Franz-Olivier Giesbert, journalist, author

Bethann Hardison

I often say, "thank goodness for Gucci and blessed am I." And often, the listener's reply will be something like "they're lucky to have you." I'm too modest to see things in quite those terms, but I will always recognize the value of Kering and be grateful that the group, and Gucci, came back into my life again in February 2019.

I'm a longtime Gucci admirer. My first exposure to the House was sometime in the mid-seventies, over lunch with my friend Michael Coady, then the executive editor of *Women's Wear Daily*, and Aldo Gucci. I was a little intimidated so I'd just sit and listen, which is how I learned, for example, that the Gucci flagship on Fifth Avenue in New York would close for two hours every afternoon, per the custom in Italy. No other store in the city did that. I've always been impressed by non-conformists. As a young Black girl from Brooklyn, I immediately became a fan of Aldo Gucci because he was not only kind but also made me feel like I belonged. Throughout the years, my fandom endured—for the designers, most of the time, but above all for the House's legacy.

I've always been an activist for racial diversity in fashion. Even in recent history, there have been times when brands were blatantly, seemingly obliviously, coming up short. I didn't want to tussle with the only luxury brand that I cared about personally, but I was prepared to do so. Over the past decade or so, I've circled back to the brand and gotten to know Kering better. I sensed a new energy, appreciated the brand's sincere commitment to honoring many beauties, and admired how it has achieved a cultural relevance few others can rival.

While diversity in fashion has changed for the better over the past decade, I still believe there's room for improvement across the industry. That is why it's important for me, in my work as a consultant, to engage with people and brands that dare to make a difference. Being a member of the Gucci Changemakers Council and becoming the Executive Advisor for Global Equity and Culture Engagement at Gucci has opened my eyes to the group's ambitious goals and all that is being achieved through engaging with students and communities on a grassroots level. Wanting to give back in such an extremely conscious way, supporting local organizations, and living your commitments are all essential to doing right, now and in the future. In my work with the Gucci Design Fellowship Program, I've gotten to know fashion students from around the world and watched them grow in their year spent in the design studio in Rome. Seeing them blossom gives me hope for the future. On Kering's watch, fashion is improving on every level, over and above the financial success of the group's individual brands. I take my hat off to François-Henri Pinault for his leadership, and to Marco Bizzarri for his tenure at Gucci. Being in the company of "do-ers" who are invested in the global issues that affect people everywhere and our planet is for me a source of great personal pride. Above all, I am grateful to know I am seen and heard, and I'm inspired to watch—from a front-row perch—the enormous differences being made in our lifetime.

Bethann Hardison, model, advocate, film director

Ghada Hatem

When I set out on the Maison des Femmes adventure in 2012, I knew nothing about the world of associations and even less about sponsorship. The Kering Foundation, through its executive director, was the first foundation to believe in our project.

The meeting didn't happen by chance, though: as always, a slight alignment of the planets made it happen. The Kering Foundation understood the convergence of its engagement and values and the mission that the Maison des Femmes has set for itself: to provide a central point for resources to address the needs of vulnerable women and victims of violence.

And it is no surprise that the Kering Foundation is currently the most committed to helping us spread our model throughout France. It is a major force behind the sponsorship program that has been established in its wake, and plays an integral part in evaluating and validating various projects undertaken by healthcare organizations looking to join our Re#Start collective.

Kering is helping us lead this national collective, to organize our outreach in France, and to define the evaluation criteria that should, in time, enable us to measure our impact and urge the government to fulfill its sovereign role: the care and support of victims of violence.

We have had several opportunities to present our development projects to the Foundation's Board of Directors, and have always been pleasantly surprised by the warm welcome we've received. François-Henri Pinault has even given us his personal commitment to the causes we defend.

For me, three memories illustrate this atypical partnership between an association and the Foundation that supports it:

When we presented the figures regarding incest in France to the Board, Mr. Pinault immediately made the link with violence against women and expressed his support to open a dedicated clinic at the Maison des Femmes.

When one of the Kering Foundation's board meetings was held at the Maison des Femmes, I was very touched to hear Mr. Pinault, a little emotional, say how he was looking forward to visiting the project they had supported for the first time.

Finally, and not least, Salma Hayek Pinault's participation in a discussion group for victims of female circumcision, and her emancipatory speech that galvanized them, remain for our patients a highlight of their stay at the Maison des Femmes.

The support I have received from the Foundation's professionals has made it possible for me to gradually find my feet and develop our association, which is now recognized as being in the public interest.

Together, we hope to support the opening of fifteen new Maisons des Femmes by the end of 2026.

*Gadha Hatem, gynecologist, obstetrician, founder
and head doctor, La Maison des Femmes in Saint-Denis*

François Henrot

For almost forty years, I have worked with and for the group built by François Pinault and now expanded by François-Henri, in three successive configurations: as a partner, a director, and as a senior banker.

In each of these positions, and over the years, I have been able to see the powerful, consistent genes in his specific DNA, which explains his extraordinary success.

For the Compagnie Bancaire, which I managed alongside his chairman, André Lévy-Lang, the Pinault-Printemps-Redoute group was a demanding, impatient partner, tough in negotiations but loyal and dependable, whose boss, François Pinault, said what he thought and did what he said. The bond of trust and mutual esteem that grew between us led François Pinault to ask me to sit on PPR's Supervisory Board. I remained for fourteen years and was lucky enough to see up close the strategic shift that took the company from a French-centered consumer retailer to a global luxury group. The change was inspired by intuition and not by reports from consultants, and was carried out with a stupefying blend of empiricism, opportunities seized at lightning speed, and a method of learning and disseminating knowledge across the group that is not only different but even opposed to mass-market retailing. I'll never forget the emergency board meeting for the ratification of Gucci's acquisition, a striking illustration of Napoleon's celebrated dictum: "In battle, first you engage, then you see!"

Other of the group's traits then became apparent: its audacity, its agility, and its ability to take risks, preferring, in an American way, an imperfect quick decision to a fully analyzed but much slower one. A corporate culture founded on proven confidence and in our ability to resolve problems as they arise!

During these years of transformation, François Pinault entrusted me with several mandates to sell his "historical" businesses, his credit subsidiary Rexel, Printemps, etc., always with valuation objectives resembling the north face of Annapurna and always with the same demand for speed in execution! In our country, where the tempo of business, no doubt influenced by the weight of the state in the economy and by our long history, is more often an andante than a scherzo, the rapidity of movement is a significant competitive advantage, much more so than in other developed economies. And I have never seen another group where the speed is as great as in the Pinault group!

But for Kering's acquisitions in the luxury industry, as Artémis's in the fine wines sector, the group has been able to adapt to the characteristics of the different sectors and to "take the time to take time," accepting, not without occasional impatience, that seeds sown can take years to germinate, and to rediscover, intact, the partnership culture of its early days, demonstrating again and again its respect for minority partners, its loyalty and commitment, and its sense of the long-term, an approach that, as everyone can see in the luxury industry as elsewhere, is rare—and distinctive!

When I helped the group through the financial crisis of 2008 and 2009, when its longstanding banking partners were at his heels, forcing him to sell his saleable assets in a panic: his "strength" in the face of hardship was like a menhir that no pressure can shift.

Throughout these four decades, the incredibly singular spirit of its founder has inspired the group, which has been passed on to his son, who now runs it. It is a spirit made up of a farmer's realism, free of illusions, but also the capacity to dream of the future, a fighting spirit energized by adversity, but also an unfailing loyalty to staff and partners, a demand for speed that neither the years nor success has tempered, but also the capacity to see and act for the long-term. A remarkable alliance of opposites!

For all those who work for him and for those that have supported him, these last forty years have been one of the most exhilarating entrepreneurial adventures of our day.

François Henrot, special senior adviser, Rothschild & Co.

Hung Huang

Almost ten years ago, I was offered the rare opportunity to interview François-Henri Pinault. Seizing this chance, I was excited as I prepared questions about his vision for the luxury industry and the newly named Kering group.

The day of the interview, Beijing was under smog so thick you could taste it. As we talked, Mr. Pinault politely answered my questions, but eventually, he asked me, "Can we talk about something very close to my heart? But it has nothing to do with marketing."

He began explaining his vision of a sustainable company with sustainable brands. He talked about a collaboration with an Italian university to create a new technology for leather treatment, one that requires no heavy metals; having visited many tanning factories in China, I knew the process creates horrific soil pollution. He also outlined the recently introduced Environmental Profit & Loss Account (EP&L). This system ensures that all Kering's fundamentals are measured by the environmental footprint of its activities and not just financial profits. I was amazed. There is a lot of talk about environmental concerns, but I had never heard an execution plan as detailed as Kering's. It was clear that Mr. Pinault was committed to this agenda. In answer to my question about how his executives reacted to these new standards, he told me he had personally visited every brand to explain the concept. He was pleasantly surprised; he found everyone was on the same wavelength and ready to commit.

Mr. Pinault asked me whether I thought Chinese companies would be as eager to engage. My response was not very positive. At the time, most Chinese companies were still preoccupied with profit and cash flow.

"Kering cannot achieve its goals alone. We need our suppliers to join us," he told me. Since our conversation, over the intervening decade, Kering has set up free online courses to teach sustainable design; it has established the Kering Generation Award to support sustainable fashion start-ups, and Mr. Pinault himself has visited China numerous times to participate in seminars and to chair the jury for the Kering Generation Award.

These efforts have not been in vain. Inspired by Kering's leadership in sustainability, Chinese fashion brands are following the group's lead. Many are focusing on upcycling material while others are exploring alternative fashion, including vintage and upcycling. In 2022, Kering hosted a packed sustainability forum at Shanghai Fashion Week.

There is a saying in Chinese: 星星之火可以燎原 / "A single spark can light up the meadow." Kering is the spark lighting the way for fashion sustainability.

Hung Huang, author, publisher, actress

Bernard-Henri Lévy

I have so many memories with François, it is as if we have lived
a thousand lives. So, for now, just an image. Just one. My father had
just died. François is one of the first people I see after several
weeks shut away in mourning. It is very early in the morning. We're
alone on the second floor of Le Flore, where we've become regulars.
He finds simple words that bring a little comfort. He remembers
the happy days when the two of them controlled the world of wood
and its métiers. He remembers Bécob, their respectful rivalry,
the forebear's cold war, the "old lion" he faced for so long, and
finally, their friendship. And then there is a more mundane subject
we have to discuss: my film, *Day and Night*, which they'd decided
to produce together and that my father had already put on track
with enthusiasm and faith; now that he's no longer here, I have
neither the energy nor the will. There's a long silence. He stares
at me with his piercing blue eyes. An air of almost joyful defiance,
the meaning of which I don't then understand. And finally, this
admonishment, not supplicating, very gentle: "Well, you're wrong.
It is exactly because he is no longer here and because he wanted
this to happen that we have to go on. We must, no matter the cost,
see it through; and I will, without him and for him, as a tribute and
out of loyalty, take over." Word kept. Lauren Bacall ... Alain Delon ...
The hell of filming in Mexico ... Insurance that doesn't cover hot-air
ballooning accidents ... Fevers, good and bad ... Tricky things ...
Drama ... He would tackle it all, head-on. Taking on everything.
He would live this unreasonable adventure, that we would ultimately
dedicate to the memory of the Absent, for two. And he would
still be there, by my side, when the film was released, and continuing
along its ill-fated path, received the inauspicious reception
we all know.

This is one story among many. There are happier ones that I will, one day, give the fate they deserve. And there are still others, from later, when he became the sovereign of the global empire that he built alone, whose dazzling success we celebrate here, and which, like all founders of dynasties, he passed on to his son François-Henri. But for me, this vignette says it all. It introduces everything. For it was here that our unique brotherhood was forged, one that time has not diminished. He was always there for me. And I, in my own way, for him. Here, there are two musketeers. All is fair in love and war. And life and death.

Bernard-Henri Lévy, philosopher

Alain Minc

When François Pinault acquired Printemps in the fall of 1991, after a night of negotiation, I understood his entrepreneurial DNA. He called me at 11am, as he was walking out of the store, furious at the nonchalance of the shop assistants he was testing by pretending to be a hesitant buyer of a tie. And the end of the conversation was: what are we going to buy now?

He brought the same energy to "upsetting the apple cart" and scuppering the absurd deal Crédit Lyonnais had made to sell FNAC. The "apple"—FNAC—fell into his lap.

I remember, a few years later, the stunned looks on the faces of the directors who had been urgently brought together to approve the acquisition of Gucci and Yves Saint Laurent, names they only knew from their Christmas shopping.

Buying at speed is an art, but so is selling at the right time. That's how I remember François Pinault's complete lack of nostalgia about selling his timber business, the origin of his success, to a German buyer.

Intuition and fast action have transformed a group that was born in the timber industry, moved through distribution and retail, and is flourishing in luxury goods. But it would not have happened without the clinical dispassion to leave a beloved industry once convinced that its decline was inevitable and it had to be abandoned at full speed. But corporate life has its own rhythm: after the emotion of strategizing comes the resolve of the managers. When I see François-Henri inaugurate Gucci or Saint Laurent stores, I remember the young man he used to be, showing me around the dingy warehouses of Pinault Distribution, timber specialists, and explaining the laughable returns from the associated sectors. It's only when you've grasped the rigors of management necessary to reach 2 or 3 percent profit that you can end up running companies with enormous margins without getting overwhelmed by the madness of numbers and appearances. Like breathing in and out, success in business requires the perspective of a strategist and then the Penelope-like work of the manager.

Over the course of a generation, Kering has benefited, in their proper order, from both.

Alain Minc, economist, essayist

Paul Polman

Kering has long been a sustainability pioneer, and in an industry in which such tendencies don't always come automatically. The company has raised industry standards for what responsible behavior should look like, not least through its flagship Gucci brand. Kering's decision to develop and share its Environmental Profit & Loss account, to measure the environmental impact of its activities, not only helped it rethink the businesses' impact on the wider world, but also helped raise awareness across the sector.

François-Henri Pinault, a dear friend and true leader, has always understood the value of these wider mindset shifts: no company can fix our shared societal and environmental problems alone. We need entire industries to move, and fashion must move further and faster than most. I therefore agreed immediately when François-Henri asked me to co-chair with him a collective of fashion companies, following a request from President Macron. The Fashion Pact now comprises around 80 companies, representing 250 brands, and accounts for nearly

30 percent of the industry; it is working collectively to transform fashion, putting its businesses in greater service of people and planet. There is no other industry coalition like it, and the potential for change is immense. François-Henri has himself set an extraordinary example. Leading with humility and humanity, his propensity for action and his focus on results are a lesson to all.

Paul Polman, business leader, campaigner,
and coauthor of Net Positive:
How Courageous Companies Thrive
by Giving More Than They Take

Xavier Romatet

François-Henri and I met at HEC, from which we graduated in 1986. At that time, he was a halfway decent soccer player, and if I remember correctly played rugby beside Jean-François Palus, now number two at Kering and a formidable linchpin.

Our paths have crossed ever since, as our professional lives have evolved.

I remember our first collaboration very well. At the time, I had just launched a communications agency, Directing, and François-Henri asked me to come and see him in Cholet, in a Pinault Bois & Matériaux branch he was running. With conviction, passion, and immense detail, he explained to me how the company, its stores, and warehouses worked. My mission was to create traffic in the various sales outlets.

Several years later, after I'd sold my agency to the communications group DDB, François-Henri, who had become Chairman of Fnac, asked me to work on the company's communication strategy, the specifics of its positioning, and the values it wanted to project. He was already passionate about technology and convinced that technological objects would soon become cultural assets: this was in 1997. By the way, during our presentation the projection equipment malfunctioned. With just a few clicks and reconnections, François-Henri was able to put everything right.

In 2006, I took over as chairman of the Condé Nast media group. At the time, I was hesitant and asked François-Henri for advice; he had taken over as chairman of Kering (then PPR) a few months earlier. He encouraged me to accept the position by sharing his vision of fashion's evolution, in which Kering would become a major player. During the thirteen years I spent at Condé Nast, François-Henri never made any remarks, pressure, or requests concerning the editorial treatment of his group's brands, in *Vogue* and the other magazines I oversaw.

In 2019, when I was asked to lead the Institut Français de la Mode and transform it into the world's leading fashion school, I was again encouraged by François-Henri. To raise funding for research and the evolution of teaching, we are developing a program of chairs. For the one related to sustainability, François-Henri immediately agreed to make Kering a partner. He then went on to explain how sustainability will be a central, indispensable part of transforming the fashion industry, for all stakeholders.

These are just a few examples I have seen in my professional life of François-Henri's vision, commitment, and availability. He is able to combine professional rigor and personal warmth, clarity of thought and relevance of ideas, trust and humanity.

These are the values I think are important to him and that, from the outside, constitute how we feel about this group.

Xavier Romatet, Dean, Institut Français de la Mode

Serge Weinberg

The story of how Kering was built is extraordinary.

Two events illustrating this singular legacy come to mind.

Of the fifteen years I spent with the group, between 1990 and 2005, two dates embody its DNA, which is inseparable from that of François Pinault and of François-Henri Pinault, and mark two pivotal stages in its development.

The first, March 16, 1990. François Pinault and I walk into the large building on Place d'Iéna that houses CFAO. Our footsteps echo in the lobby, but otherwise, total silence. For almost a year, François Pinault had been buying shares in the CFAO group and had thus become its main shareholder. Leaving the world of wood, both trade and industry, he had taken control of a conglomerate made up of a large number of companies in Africa, as well as different assets in France and the United States, a major food distribution business, La Ruche Méridionale, and several professional retail/distribution businesses, including CDME, which later became Rexel. The merger of the Pinault and CFAO groups would generate the resources to break into the consumer retail sector. Nobody saw it coming, but more than anything else, nobody had seriously looked at that group, whose poor management concealed the quality of its assets.

The second date, March 1999, when he acquired a stake in Gucci. With the swiftness of an eagle swooping on its prey, François Pinault understood immediately that acquiring a stake in Gucci like a white knight would enable him to move to a new and decisive stage in the transformation of a French, then a European company into a global player in the luxury sector. That same night, we became

Gucci's main shareholder, while Artémis's teams acquired the Yves Saint Laurent House, which was later sold to the Gucci Group. The intuition that luxury goods, a global market, was growing faster than any other business in which we were involved.

Two dates, two defining moments of audacity and courage in the pursuit of a vision, and at each step, François Pinault's often-repeated phrase "now it all begins," as if all that had gone before didn't exist.

François-Henri has been able to develop this enterprise in a way that was unimaginable when I left the group in 2005, turning it into one of the world's luxury giants, and no doubt he, too, believes that it all begins now.

Serge Weinberg, business leader

Anna Wintour

In March 2023 in Venice, I co-hosted with François and François-Henri Pinault a dinner to celebrate the opening of the exhibition *Chronorama*, at Palazzo Grassi. By any usual standard, this would have been a magical night. Yet this one was a particularly extraordinary evening for me, for *Vogue*, for the Newhouse family, and for Condé Nast, because *Chronorama* showcased many iconic and unforgettable images from our photographic archive from the last 100 years, an archive of which Pinault Collection acquired a huge swatch in 2021.

You will have to excuse me for a moment while I take some pride in witnessing the collective artistic and cultural heft of the work on display. More importantly, though, it was a powerful reminder that investing in, and understanding, the past offers the most clear-sighted way to look to the future. Not so unlike the book you're reading today.

As an editor, one's nature is always to look forward, but when I looked with awe at that exceptional collection of many of the greatest photographs of the twentieth century, I confess I felt nostalgic for a different era. I thought back to a time when Irving Penn took pictures with barely anyone around him, only an assistant, a *Vogue* editor, a model, and his exacting standards. I thought of Helmut Newton's tiny camera and his highly original point of view. I thought of how a young fashion editor would be sent on a trip for weeks with only a photographer, a model, and perhaps one hundred dollars in her pocket for expenses—"find a maharajah to put you up," she was told—and somehow came back with stories and images that astonished editors and readers alike.

It was a time of risk-taking and fearlessness and every picture in that exhibition brought me back to it. Each was an act of bravery in itself, and taken together they are nothing short of a history lesson, telling the story of the twentieth century through people, places, fashion, art, and culture. Alexander Liberman, Condé Nast's legendary editorial director, commissioned so much of the work that it contains. "Choose the pictures that burn the page," he'd always say.

A few years ago, Condé Nast received a call that Monsieur François Pinault, the great collector and philanthropist, wished to see the company's archives. He arrived just like Mr. Penn: perfectly on time, with one other colleague. I had cleared my entire morning but François spent maybe ten minutes examining our treasures before giving a brief nod to his associate and silently departing. His generous (and swift) decision to give such an extraordinary home to our archives will give generations to come not only enormous pleasure but also a deeper understanding of the golden age of photography.

Anna Wintour, Condé Nast
and Global Editorial Director, Vogue

A MAJOR DISTRIBUTOR 1991-2003

The takeover of CFAO marked the beginning of the group's history in distribution and retail. In only a few years, Pinault SA built an empire centered around such prestigious French brands as Printemps, La Redoute, Fnac, and Conforama, as well as an electrical equipment distribution division, which became a world leader in the sector. Initially renamed Pinault-Printemps and then Pinault-Printemps-Redoute (PPR), the company continued to withdraw from the timber industry while simultaneously developing a group dynamic aimed at fostering synergies between its various businesses, creating a shared culture and strengthening its international positions. At the end of the 1990s, PPR was listed on the French stock market index CAC 40 and figured among the leading French companies. It was at this point that the chance presented itself to enter a new sector: luxury goods.

The Compagnie Française d'Afrique Occidentale (CFAO) offices in Nigeria in 1955.

BUILDING AN EMPIRE
(1991–93)

"I want to build a group of European, indeed, global dimensions, in the field of specialized distribution and services. Believe me, it's all starting now!" In an interview he gave to the magazine *L'Expansion* in September 1990—one of his first with the national press—François Pinault declared his ambitions loud and clear. After establishing the European leader in timber in less than thirty years, he was preparing to implement a radically new and equally ambitious project. And he had the solid foundations to make it happen ...

A group in search of new opportunities

In 1989, at the time he became interested in CFAO, François Pinault moved his group's headquarters from Avenue Marceau to 5 Boulevard de La Tour-Maubourg, which had previously been occupied by LVMH. This was where he would now work, surrounded by a small team, including Hervé Guillaume (general manager), Patricia Barbizet (finance and treasury), Cécile de Guillebon (development), Michel Friocourt (legal department), François-Henri Pinault, who managed France Bois Industrie (industrial woodwork), and Serge Weinberg who left Banque Pallas in 1990 to take over the management of CFAO. "François Pinault has never liked cumbersome structures, which tend to hinder operations. For him, the team working alongside him needs to be able to quickly respond to acquisitions and divestments," relates Michel Friocourt. Indeed, this small team would play a crucial role in the group's transition to retail.

In the wake of CFAO's acquisition, the Pinault SA group was organized into four divisions: specialized distribution, with Pinault Distribution (timber trade and distribution), Compagnie de Distribution de Matériel Électrique (CDME), and Compagnie Internationale de Commerce et d'Approvisionnement (wholesale automobile distribution)—these last two businesses came from CFAO; industry, with Isoroy, France Bois Industrie, and Compagnie Internationale d'Ameublement as its main companies; services with Pinault Équipement (construction equipment leasing, which came from CFAO), Transcap Logistique (road haulage and courier services, also part of CFAO), and Pinault-Services, which included the delivery and light equipment leasing services created by the group in the 1980s; and finally, international trade with CFAO. In 1991, timber activities—France Bois Industrie, Isoroy, and Compagnie Internationale d'Ameublement—were grouped together in a new holding company, Générale de Finances et de Participation (GEFIP), with the financial reins handed to Jean-François Palus, whom François-Henri Pinault had met at HEC Paris and who was then working as an auditor and financial adviser at Arthur Andersen. François-Henri Pinault took over the management of Pinault Distribution.

Within what was still in many ways a conglomerate of diverse activities, specialized distribution stood apart thanks to its size: it represented no less than 19.5 billion francs, that is, 60 percent of the group's revenue. The division mainly catered to professionals, craftsmen, and manufacturers in the construction sector, as well as resellers and car dealers. It also benefited from strong commercial positions, not only in France, but also in Europe. CDME was the second-largest French electrical distributor and one of the largest in Europe. As for Pinault Distribution, it had long been the leading European timber importer. For François Pinault, who wanted to gradually withdraw from the sector, strengthening this division, which was already well-established in its markets, was a priority. However, the entrepreneur had no intention of limiting himself to professional distribution. He had always been in fact interested in the whole distribution sector—specialized and general, professional and consumer.

The entrepreneur clearly understood this: confronted with an industry subject to growing competition from countries with low production costs and increasingly serious environmental challenges, distribution was clearly the direction to take. It had been enjoying renewed momentum since the mid-1980s, and the situation was promising. After the long recession resulting from the oil crises of 1973 and 1979, France had experienced robust economic growth since 1986, which accelerated at the end of the decade. In 1988 and 1989, for example, GDP had expanded by more than 4 percent per year. Oil prices began dropping sharply in 1986—that year, the price of a barrel of oil fell below 10 US dollars—and along with it, inflation, and these were major factors in this growth. Within this setting, from the mid-1980s, the construction industry—one of the main markets for Pinault SA's distribution division for both timber and electrical equipment—experienced vigorous recovery. People and businesses had begun building homes and offices once again. Between 1985 and 1989, the number of new homes built in France grew from 285,000 to 339,000.

François Pinault saw this as a particularly good time to strengthen his position in professional distribution. But it was also the moment to gain a foothold in consumer distribution, both specialized and general. Here again, it was a matter of context. France had been experiencing consumer fever since 1986, due mainly to the sharp drop in inflation and its impact on purchasing power. Household consumption was growing by an average of 3 percent per year. This was especially the case with household equipment—electrical appliances and furniture—but also with beauty, leisure, and culture: during the second half of the 1980s, sales grew progressively, at around 5 percent per year. Specialized stores were the undeniable winners of this growth. The very ones that François Pinault would soon take an interest in.

The entrepreneur was already very familiar with these figures. Following the CFAO takeover, he was on the lookout for opportunities that would enable him to strengthen his distribution division. The first of these was in electrical equipment, in which the Pinault group was already a major player, thanks to CDME. For some time, the sector had been experiencing radical transformation: the time had come for consolidation and internationalization. It was a time when CDME's main French competitors—Sonepar and Legrand in particular—were expanding acquisitions of independent distributors, not only in France but also elsewhere in the world. By the end of the 1980s, Sonepar was established in Italy, Switzerland, and Northern Europe, while Legrand had a foothold in the United States. CDME was also part of the sector's vast reorganization. In February 1991, it acquired the 24.5 percent stake Lyonnaise-Dumez held in Groupelec, France's third-largest electrical goods distributor, with sales of 2.1 billion francs. The construction giant had decided to sell its stake to focus on water, urban services, and the construction and public works industry. The move placed CDME on par with Sonepar, the French leader in the sector, and strengthened its position in European markets. The Pinault group had just taken a decisive step in electrical distribution. The ones that would soon follow would propel it to first European and then

101

Conforama in 1976.

Conforama in 1976.

global leadership of the sector. We will return to this. But at that moment, François Pinault was interested in another company: Conforama. With this move, the group was readying itself to enter the world of specialized consumer distribution.

A first milestone: The takeover of Conforama

It all started in September 1990, when François Pinault learned, from Crédit Lyonnais Managing Director Jean-Paul Amiel, that the furniture chain Conforama was for sale. It was then owned by Bernard Arnault, president of LVMH, who had acquired it in 1984 when he bought Financière Agache-Willot, the starting point of his adventures in the luxury sector. Seeking to concentrate solely on this sector, Bernard Arnault had decided to sell the furniture brand.

François Pinault was immediately interested. And he made it known. In an interview with *L'Expansion* in September 1990, he said, "Yes, I'm interested in this type of business; in furniture, controlling distribution is strategic." Founded in 1967 in Saint-Priest and taken over by Agache-Willot in 1976, before becoming part of LVMH, Conforama was one of the very first furniture and home equipment chains in France. In 1990, it represented 10 percent of the country's furniture market and 6 percent of its electrical appliance market. It had 147 stores, as well as the 77 stores of the brand Mobis, acquired in 1990. Altogether, the group's revenue was 7 billion francs. Buoyed by the strong economic climate and the rise in consumption, Conforama was thriving and making money. By acquiring it, the group led by François Pinault would considerably strengthen its distribution division. The deal would also increase synergies with its operations in the timber industry.

All that was left was to finalize the deal. From the beginning, Bernard Arnault set the bar high: he was ready to sell the company for 6 billion francs. François Pinault had no intention of going over 3.5 billion. It took six months for the two men to reach an agreement. In April 1991, an accord was finally reached: LVMH sold Conforama to the Pinault group for 4.4 billion francs. The financial package was, as the economic press declared, a "model of financial refinement." *Option Finance* magazine even described it as the "package of the year." The deal was carried out in several phases. The first: Le Bon Marché, a subsidiary of LVMH, holding more than an 85 percent stake in Conforama, carries out a capital increase to which the Pinault SA subsidiary Compagnie Internationale d'Ameublement, contributes. Second stage: Le Bon Marché transferred its Conforama shares to a sub-subsidiary. Third step: the Compagnie Internationale d'Ameublement exchanged its Bon Marché shares for Conforama shares. Finally, the minority shareholders in Conforama were offered cash for their shares or the chance to exchange them for Bon Marché shares. The deal was undoubtedly complex, but it ultimately revealed the extent of François Pinault's talents.

The acquisition of Conforama marked a major turning point in the group's transition to retail. Its share of Pinault SA increased significantly in comparison to the group's industrial activities. "My objective was to first be an entrepreneurial merchant, then a manufacturer, and finally a financier," declared François Pinault in the magazine *Challenges* in May 1991.

Those words say a lot about the new vocation of the group and its founder. Above all, with this deal, Pinault SA established itself as the number one furniture company in France. Conforama completed the range the company already offered, via the Compagnie Internationale d'Ameublement, in kitchen furnishings (Arthur Bonnet, Comera, Ranger, ICM), office furniture (Ordo, Trau), and for local authorities (Lafa, Mullca). "We were one of the few European groups to cover the entire timber industry, from the forest to the dining room," François Pinault pointed out in the pages of *Challenges*. Thus, the acquisition of Conforama marked the culmination of François Pinault's entrepreneurial beginnings in timber, as much as it embodied the group's new ambitions. In fact, Conforama represented only a first step. Just a few months after completing the deal, the entrepreneur took control of another well-known name in consumer retail: the French department store Printemps.

Printemps: Consolidating a mission

Once again, François Pinault stood apart for his ability to seize an opportunity when it appeared. Since 1972, when it experienced financial difficulties due to a slowdown in consumer spending, Printemps had been owned by the Swiss group Maus Frères. Under the leadership of Jean-Jacques Delort—former general manager of the Italian animal feed group Provimi, then general administrator of the Prouvost press group, who was appointed Chairman of the Board in 1977— the department store had made a strong recovery before expanding in new directions, particularly into food, with the acquisition of the Disco chain; apparel, with the takeover of Armand Thiery; and mail order with the purchase of La Redoute. Now a genuine group, Printemps also developed internationally, opening stores in Tokyo, Istanbul, Jeddah, Dubai, Singapore, and Kuala Lumpur. In the early 1990s, the company's revenue was almost 30 billion francs. Then, an unexpected event turned the tables.

In July 1991, the American subsidiary of the Maus group, which was experiencing serious financial difficulties, announced that the sixty-eight stores it managed on the other side of the Atlantic had to close and that it was thus filing for bankruptcy in the United States. With a debt of 900 million dollars, it had been hit by the rise in interest rates in America and a decline in consumption. Maus's failure on the US market gave rise to all kinds of speculation, especially concerning the future of Printemps. Rumors were soon swirling that the Swiss group intended to sell it in order to relieve its debt.

Legend has it that François Pinault heard the news on the radio while returning from Le Bourget airport after a business trip to Poland. He immediately started bidding for the company. The acquisition of Printemps offered many advantages: first, it would dramatically strengthen its distribution division, especially for consumers, which had previously been limited to Conforama. It would also allow the company to consolidate the finances of Pinault SA, which was heavily in debt. Finally, in terms of image and reputation, it would be a real shift in scale. Created in 1865, Printemps was an institution in the world of retail. Each year, hundreds of thousands of clients, from France, but ever increasingly from overseas, passed through the doors of the department store's flagship on Boulevard

Le Printemps department store, Christmas 1975.

Haussmann. With its twenty-seven floors spread over three buildings and its famous dome, it was also an iconic Parisian landmark; it was listed as a historical monument in 1975. Created amid the 1930s crisis to offer low-cost products and food, its subsidiary Prisunic was also well known. With its ninety-three stores located in city centers—a unique legacy!—and two hundred franchises, it was France's leading and most popular neighborhood store, ahead of its competitor Monoprix. And then there was La Redoute, yet another institution. Founded in Roubaix, in northern France, in 1837, it had become the leader in French mail-order services. Its 1,200-page catalog offered more than 60,000 products. You could find absolutely everything. With Printemps, the Pinault group would thus enrich its distribution division with prestigious brands that were the leaders in their respective markets.

François Pinault was, of course, not the only one interested in the retail group. Others were waiting in line, including the German companies Metro and Quelle. But the entrepreneur had two major advantages: being French, which won him the approval of the cabinet of Pierre Bérégovoy, Minister of Economy and Finance, who was keen to bring the department stores back under the country's tricolor flag; and he had the support of Jean-Jacques Delort, leader of the Printemps group, and of Jean-Paul Huchon, his number two, who were also anxious to find a French solution. Another important asset: Jean-Yves Haberer, President of Crédit Lyonnais, was ready to back him. Once again, François Pinault's longstanding bank was by his side. The entrepreneur could also count on the help and advice of a number of prominent corporate figures, particularly Ambroise Roux, who still chaired the French Association of Private Enterprises, and Alain Minc, who had just founded his own consulting firm. With François Pinault's close associates and lawyer Jean-Michel Darrois overseeing the legal aspects, the three men would play a fundamental role in the success of the deal, which of course was not without risk. The Printemps group was a large part of the equation, with revenue equal to two-thirds of that of Pinault SA. To take control, the group would have to pay a little more than 5 billion francs, which could well have considerably increased its debt, and in so doing, caused concern among financial analysts. It would finally be up to François Pinault's advisers to refine the financial aspects of the deal, to ensure that the acquisition of Printemps would have a limited impact on Pinault SA's balance sheet. As for Ambroise Roux, with the support of his many contacts he worked to reassure the financial community and emphasize the soundness of François Pinault's project.

At the end of September 1991, the latter's offer was widely seen to be favored over that of its competitors, which included the French group Euris, led by Jean-Charles Naouri, who had also entered the fray. However, it was not until November 26, 1991, that the negotiations with the Maus and Nordmann families finally came to an end. On that day, François Pinault officially announced the acquisition of the Printemps group by Pinault SA. The latter would initially buy the 40.56 percent stake that Maus-Nordmann held in Printemps for 3.3 billion francs. A takeover bid would then be launched to increase this stake to 66 percent. In a third phase, Printemps would buy Conforama from Pinault SA, enabling the latter to complete the deal without significantly increasing its debt level. With excellent advice, François Pinault had proved, yet again, his immense financial creativity.

Acquiring Conforama was an essential step in the development of Pinault SA's distribution division; the takeover of Printemps was even more important! In terms of sales, the transaction represented a significant jump: overnight, the numbers increased from 40 to 70 billion francs. It also accelerated the group's conversion to distribution and retail, which now represented 80 percent of Pinault SA's revenue, 54 percent of which was consumer retail. With its Conforama, Printemps, Prisunic, Armand Thiery, and La Redoute brands, the group no longer sold only furniture and appliances to the public, as was the case with Conforama. Through direct sales and mail order, it now offered a wide range of products, from clothing to food, as well as beauty, lifestyle, fashion, small and large household appliances, toys, and even gardening equipment. This remarkable transformation made Pinault SA the number two retailer in Europe, behind Germany's Quelle. The change also enabled the group to become familiar with new product categories and consumer behaviors. Such product knowledge was very new for the group and would not go to waste. The time was now right for it to organize and restructure its various activities.

Restructuring: The creation of Artémis and the founding of the Pinault-Printemps group

"We will withdraw from certain activities that have become marginal or which don't show enough profit, and in which we have no real growth prospects," warned François Pinault the day after he announced his takeover bid for Printemps. In fact, at the end of 1991, implementing a divestment program became necessary. Even though the group's debt was contained because of its many acquisitions since 1990, it remained high. While observers were sometimes concerned by this, François Pinault was more serene. If he had taken on debt, it was for a good reason: to grow his group. On November 26, 1991, he explained it directly on air with Europe 1. "I much prefer to be in the position of an entrepreneur taking the initiative than being in the position of a company director watching over his money, looking at interest rate fluctuations every morning," he told journalist Jean-Pierre Elkabbach when asked about the situation. But beyond the financial dimension, which was clearly important, the withdrawal from a number of business sectors reflected the group's desire to refocus on retail, which had been clear since the takeover of CFAO. In this, François Pinault was demonstrating true strategic consistency.

Things were going well. In the wake of the acquisition of Printemps, the Pinault SA group reorganized once again—still around four branches but with revised perimeters: the consumer distribution branch (with Conforama and Printemps); the electrical appliance distribution branch, with CDME and a 24.5 percent stake in Groupelec; the manufacturing and trade branch, made up of Générale de Finances et de Participation (GEFIP) and mainly centered on timber; and the automobile distribution branch. Most of the divestments made since 1991 were connected to the manufacturing and trade division. This is not surprising: in August 1990, the First Gulf War slowed the construction market sharply. After strong growth in the second half of the 1980s, the timber subsidiary entered a new period of recession. Competition from Asian producers—not new but intensifying—aggravated the situation, as did the public's growing aversion to exotic woods of which Pinault SA was a major importer. For all these reasons, the group accelerated its withdrawal from the timber industry and, more

Top: The iconic Conforama store near the Pont-Neuf in Paris in 1993.
Bottom: The Printemps department store on Boulevard Haussmann in Paris in 1986.

particularly, from furniture production. In addition, the margins were not high. However, the company kept Conforama, part of the consumer retail sector, which remained strategic.

Thus, over the course of 1992, Pinault SA successively sold its activities in kitchen, office, and corporate furnishings, but most importantly, the wood panel manufacturer Isoroy, which it had acquired in 1986. This company, which employed 2,700 people and had 2.2 billion francs in revenue, was taken over by the European market leader, the German company Glunz, for 1.5 billion francs. With this deal, a page of the group's history was turning: Pinault SA's manufacturing presence was now only marginal. Divestments also happened in other operational branches: Transcap Logistique, which specialized in road haulage and courier services, was sold to the Sanara transport group, and the furniture chain Mobis, a subsidiary of Conforama, was taken over by the Vieux Chêne group. Conforama would now sell furniture under its own name. A short time later, in early 1993, Armand Thiery was sold to the Bidermann group. This program would continue at a steady pace in the following years. But by the beginning of 1993, the Pinault group had already streamlined its operations considerably and reduced its debt significantly.

Changing the group's name was also part of the desire for clarification. In this regard, the decisive step was taken on December 11, 1992, when Pinault SA merged with Printemps, forming the Pinault-Printemps group. With this new name, the company clearly expressed its mission: distribution and retail. This major operation was preceded by an equally important event, announced three days earlier, on December 8, 1992, and closely linked to it: the creation of the family holding company. Dubbed Artémis—the mythological goddess of hunting and nature—and headed by Patricia Barbizet, it was held by the Pinault family at 75.5 percent, with Crédit Lyonnais controlling the other 24.5 percent. Artémis held a 39.6 percent stake in Pinault-Printemps with 50.2 percent of the voting rights. The Pinault family was strengthening its control over the group that François Pinault had created and which he had transformed into one of France's leading companies. But the businessman was also providing himself with the means to continue investing in sectors other than distribution and retail. In addition, a short time earlier, he had organized his legacy, in the event of his untimely death. This was the purpose of Pinault Trustee, created in April 1992. Made up of figures in whom François Pinault had complete trust—in particular Jérôme Monod of Lyonnaise des Eaux, Alain Minc and John Ryan, who had been by his side during the Canadian timber adventures—this structure's objective was to manage François-Henri Pinault's transition as he proved himself in succeeding his father. "It was a group of trusted people whose mission was to follow my progress if something happened to my father and decide if I was fit to take over the company. It was a way of underlining that my name did not automatically make me my father's successor," explains François-Henri Pinault. While ultimately, Pinault Trustee was not required, the approach is testament to François Pinault's desire for his company to continue after his passing.

Preceded by a takeover of 33 percent of Printemps that Pinault SA did not yet control, the creation of the Pinault-Printemps group on December 11, 1992, resulted in the leading retailer in France. It had a Board, chaired by Jean-Jacques Delort, and a supervisory board, chaired by François Pinault, assisted by Ambroise Roux. The daily running of the group was in the hands of four men and one woman: Jean-Paul Huchon,

CEO; Patricia Barbizet, Deputy CEO; Serge Weinberg, CEO of CDME; Hervé Guillaume, appointed head of GEFIP; and François-Henri Pinault, CEO of Pinault-Distribution. These five executives made up the group's management committee. Their major tasks included continuing the restructuring and strengthening of the retail and distribution division, developing a shared culture, and significantly increasing the proportion of revenue generated outside France, which was 23 percent at that time.

S. WEINBERG

Pages 110-111: The decorated cupola of the Printemps
department store on Boulevard Haussmann, Paris.
Above: François-Henri Pinault and Serge Weinberg, CEO of PPR,
presenting financial results for the first half of the year 2000.

La Redoute's historic building in Roubaix.

PINAULT-PRINTEMPS-REDOUTE, A NEW RETAIL GIANT

A new period of organization began with the formation of Pinault-Printemps. From 1993, a vast effort was made to harmonize the group's activities, culminating in the creation, in 1994, of Pinault-Printemps-Redoute. Now a European retail giant, the group strengthened its position in spectacular fashion by completing a fresh major acquisition: Fnac.

A period of organization

At the dawn of 1993, despite the sales that had been made in recent months and the acceleration in refocusing on distribution and retail, Pinault-Printemps remained characterized by the diversity of its activities: consumer retailing, and professional and electrical appliance distribution, as well as that of automobiles and construction equipment; timber trading; international trade, particularly textiles with Africa; financial services, and more. All of this was managed with immense flexibility and with very little intention, until that time, to make use of the synergies between the various businesses. A characteristic that owes much to the temperament of François Pinault and his approach to management. Since founding his company in 1962, he had managed by trusting the men and women with whom he worked, giving them considerable responsibility. As a result, the group functioned in a decentralized fashion and with few multifunctional tools. "In fact, it was an aggregate of entities with a large degree of autonomy. Managers were not totally independent, but they had a lot of freedom in their actions. The advantage of this was a very fluid structure that made it easy to move the various entities within the group. As the company had grown considerably since the end of the 1980s, internal reorganization had become necessary. Shared tools had to be put in place. This was one of the major challenges of the period that began in 1993," according to Jean-François Palus.

A newcomer to Pinault-Printemps, Pierre Blayau was entrusted with the vital task of putting the group in order. An inspector of finance, former general manager and then CEO of Saint-Gobin Pont-à-Mousson (PAM), Blayau was asked by François Pinault to take over the presidency of the group's Board, previously occupied by Jean-Jacques Delort, in February 1993. "Having spent ten years in a company specialized in the manufacture of water supply pipes, I didn't know very much about retail and distribution. But François Pinault was not looking for an industry specialist. He wanted an operational manager capable of structuring the group. My mission was to bring teams together and optimize the performance of various activities through the implementation of synergies while taking into account the independence of the brands, which were major brands," he explains today. One of his first decisions was to recruit a general secretary to oversee financial, legal, tax, and real estate matters across brands. He also hired a communications director who would operate across the entire group.

Synergies were implemented rapidly. A joint purchasing policy was established across several brands for linen, small furnishings and electrical appliances, and fragrance and hygiene products, while Conforama and Fnac instigated shared sourcing for brown (electrical) goods, and Prisunic and La Redoute did the same for apparel. Finally, a number of functions—including transport, telecommunications, and supplier listing—came under central management. Through developing internal collaborations like this, Pierre Blayau intended to take the Pinault-Printemps group beyond the simple cohabitation of brands. The twin objective was to reduce costs and stream-line the company's operational methods, to make them more fluid and efficient. This strategy quickly paid off: by the end of 1993, Pinault-Printemps's debt had fallen significantly, to 13 billion francs versus almost 18 billion two years earlier.

At the same time, the activities of the different divisions making up the group were undergoing massive changes. Some were thoroughly restructured, while others were sold and new acquisitions made in key sectors. Here too, there was a group rationale at work. The aim was to better coordinate the companies, to direct investments toward growth sectors or sectors that corresponded to the group's new mission, and to optimize financial structures. All Pinault-Printemps businesses were involved. At the head of Pinault Distribution since 1991, François-Henri Pinault had been scrutinizing all the channels on which the timber trade had been based since the 1970s. "Pinault Distribution was a real challenge for me. It was the group's largest branch. It was also historic. Many of my father's former associates were still working there. But the crisis that hit in the early 1990s weakened our activities in the timber industry. We had to reorganize the agencies one by one. In the space of three years, I carried out between forty and fifty restructuring plans," he recalls. Under his leadership, Pinault Distribution was also growing new markets, especially timber for garden decoration—from stakes to pergolas—outdoor toys, and shelters. To supply these markets, a dedicated processing site had been opened in northern France.

In 1994, after successfully putting Pinault Distribution back in order, François-Henri Pinault was appointed head of CFAO. With his general manager Stephen Decam, they made multiple visits to Africa, a continent still unfamiliar to him, to meet local teams—"adventurers who knew their markets perfectly and were incredibly committed to the company," he says. He also had plans to sell certain operations, including textiles, and to study growth opportunities. It was within this framework that the takeover of Europharma, the leading distributor of pharmaceutical products in Africa and a subsidiary of the Société Commerciale de l'Ouest Africain (SCOA), was initiated in 1994; the deal was finalized in 1996. Like his father before him, in succeeding with this deal, François-Henri Pinault had reaffirmed CFAO's ties with Africa. Major restructuring was also carried out within Générale de Finances et de Participations (GEFIP), led by Hervé Guillaume. In a continuation of the divestments begun in 1991, the automobile distribution division and the construction equipment business were sold in 1993, the former to Jardine Matheson, and the latter to Bergerat Monnoyeur.

In the field of electrical distribution, on the other hand, it was time for conquest. Led by Serge Weinberg, who took the helm in 1990, the Compagnie de Matériel Électrique (CDME) was making a series of acquisitions with the goal of establishing itself as the European leader and a global player in the industry. International expansion was clearly a priority. "In the electrical material market, every company sells the same products. It's therefore difficult to gain market share solely through internal growth. The industry was also experiencing a twofold movement of consolidation and internalization. To grow, we needed to take control of brands and retail outlets that already had an identity and strong positions in the major expanding markets of Europe, North America, and Asia. Several dozen acquisitions were made in the space of three or four years," explains Serge Weinberg. Outside France, the most significant takeovers included those of the German firms Klein and Elektro-Union, the British retailer STC, the Canadian group Guillevin, and the

40 percent stake in the American group Willcox & Gibbs. CDME consolidated its position in France, increasing its stake in Groupelec to 49 percent in 1993. Following this deal, a new holding company was created, regrouping the electrical distribution activities of the Pinault-Printemps group. Dubbed Rexel, it immediately became the industry's European leader, with sales of around 18 billion francs, 50 percent of which was international. Electrical equipment was the main driving force behind the group's internationalization.

A new group: Pinault-Printemps-Redoute

By the beginning of 1994, the process of consolidating the activities of Pinault-Printemps, led by Pierre Blayau, was already well underway. In the space of a year, the group had changed enormously: it had pursued the policy of disposing of nonstrategic assets, restructuring its business divisions, consolidating its international positions, especially for electrical equipment; improved its financial structure; and instigated a number of synergies between the group's various brands. With the grouping of certain functions, the creation of shared tools, particularly in the legal, financial, and fiscal fields, and the exchange of information and expertise, a group logic had begun to be set in place, a dynamic that took on a new momentum starting in 1995.

Better organized and better structured, Pinault-Printemps was no longer the aggregate of autonomous entities existing side by side that it had been in the early 1990s. By promoting internal collaboration, it improved both its efficacy and strength. Despite its size, it remained very much characterized by a decentralized culture established by François Pinault. This was as the entrepreneur wanted it, recommending to Pierre Blayau that he "take into account the independence of each brand." In the headquarters, less than one hundred people were working directly for the Pinault-Printemps holding company. The business units and their managers maintained considerable operational latitude.

On May 18, 1994, Pinault-Printemps merged with La Redoute, creating Pinault-Printemps-Redoute, one of Europe's leading specialist retailers with revenue of just over 60 billion francs (the group would quickly be called PPR, even though it wouldn't become its official name before 2005). The deal marked a crucial step in the group's structuring. Pierre Blayau explained it clearly in the economic press, saying: "This is François Pinault's project. It is a major step in the process of creating a large, modern retail company. The group must be built on two principles. Firstly, it must prioritize the decentralization of the commercial management and running the brands and companies, allowing the group to be commercially aggressive through listening to consumer needs in terms of services, quality, and price. Secondly, we need to maximize the size effect of the brands and pool their strengths in purchasing, logistics, IT, advertising, and financial resources. By proposing a 100 percent stake in La Redoute, we are making it easier for the mail-order company and Pinault-Printemps to make the required transition from cohabitation to cooperation." By adding the name of the Northern French giant to its own—with its 15,000 employees and revenue of 18 billion francs—the company was clearly reasserting its ambitions to complete its conversion to retail and distribution and to establish itself as a global player in its various activities. The acquisition of Fnac, two months after the creation of PPR, would mark another important step in this project.

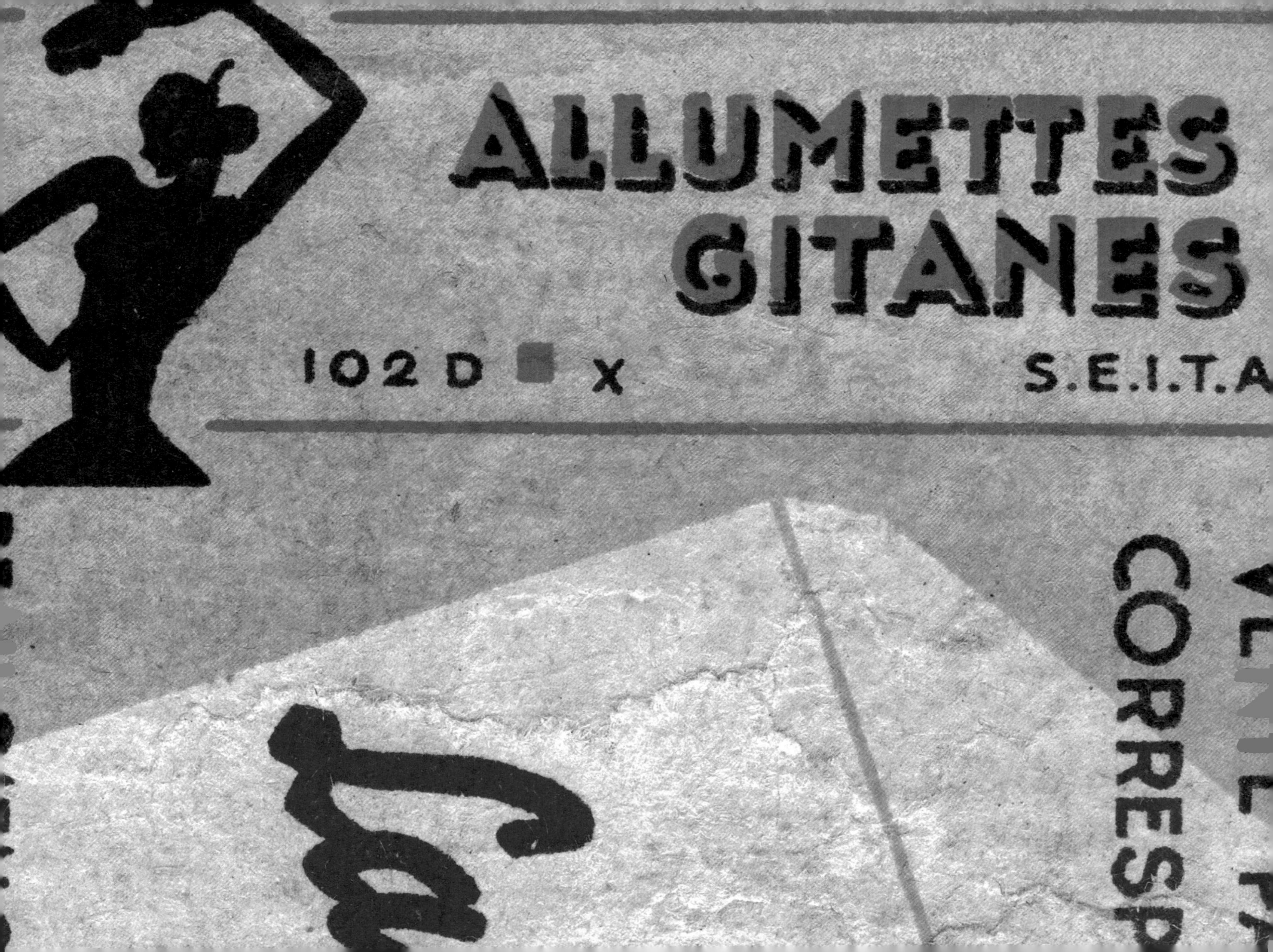
ALLUMETTES
GITANES
102 D X
S.E.I.T.A
CORRESP

NDANCE

Redoute

à Roubaix

SOUS-VÊTEMENTS, CHAUSSURES, LINGERIE, ET

Conquering Fnac

By 1994, François Pinault had already been interested in Fnac for more than a year and, in early 1993, he had met Garantie Mutuelle des Fonctionnaires (GMF) CEO Jean-Louis Petriat, who had bought Fnac in 1985. At the time, the business world was abuzz with all kinds of rumors about the cultural brand's probable sale by the mutual insurance company, which was in financial difficulty following risky investments in the hotel industry. François Pinault offered Jean-Louis Pétriat 3 billion francs for the brand.

The appeal of the deal was obvious for the Breton entrepreneur: founded in 1954 by two former left-wing activists keen to "return power to consumers," this company, unlike any other, had become an institution in the retailing of cultural products. With its fifty or so stores and annual revenue of around 9 billion francs in the early 1990s, the company was France's leading bookstore and the number one record store, two markets that were steadily expanding. It was also well-established in video, sound, and personal computing. Its acquisition would strengthen the Pinault group's consumer retail division, which at that point included Printemps, Prisunic, Conforama, and La Redoute. With Fnac's significant growth potential, the merger made all the more sense, especially internationally, where the company's presence was limited. But Jean-Louis Pétriat declared that he did not want to sell.

The matter resurfaced on July 12, 1993. On that day, François Pinault was stunned to discover that GMF had finally decided to sell Fnac. The buyer was Altus Finance, a subsidiary of Crédit Lyonnais, which for this operation had joined forces with Compagnie Immobilière Phénix (CIP), itself a subsidiary of Compagnie Générale des Eaux. To say that François Pinault was stung by the news would be an understatement. Firstly, because Altus and CIP's offering price was far lower than what he had proposed, 2.4 billion francs against 3 billion, and secondly, because Altus Finance—a subsidiary of his long-term bank—avoided apprising him of its intentions. For the two buyers, the affair quickly descended into confusion when it became known, less than a week after they had taken control, that Altus had entrusted Fnac's management to four businessmen, including two former employees of François Pinault, who had the possibility of gradually increasing their stake in the company. Was the rapid sale of Fnac, at a very advantageous price for the buyers, designed to block François Pinault's bid, which was no secret? Was Altus acting as the financier for the four businessmen? Did it have the go-ahead from its parent company to make the deal? These were just some of the questions being asked in the press.

François Pinault decided not to let it happen. For days, he held intensive meetings with Jean-Yves Haberer, who would be president of Crédit Lyonnais for a few more months, and with Guy Dejouany, CEO of Générale des Eaux, in order to put an end to the deal. And it worked: on July 24, 1993, the bank reneged on its subsidiary, before announcing twelve months later—the minimum legal period a company must be owned before it can be resold—that it was selling the 64.6 percent stake that Altus Finance held in Fnac to Artémis. Compagnie Générale des Eaux sold its 34 percent in 1997. For François Pinault, it was a triumph. "I fought like a lion," he told the press, recounting the deal's ups and downs. In fact, for a year, the entrepreneur had been completely absorbed with the operation, determined to add Fnac to his empire. As he had done since 1962, he spared no effort in achieving his goals. And he succeeded.

Voici Jean-Luc.

Il vient à la Fnac depuis qu'il est tout petit.

C'est avec nous qu'il s'est découvert
une passion pour la BD,

Tous nos vendeurs le connaissent
et le conseillent depuis des années.

Il est le premier au courant des nouveautés.

Mais aujourd'hui, ce qui nous ferait
plaisir à nous, à la Fnac,

ce serait que Jean-Luc nous achète
enfin quelque chose.

Nous avons tous les livres
Vous avez toutes les libertés

www.fnac.fr

Pages 118-119: Advertising for La Redoute on a Gitanes matchbox, c. 1930.
Above: The celebrated Fnac advertising campaign created in 1998.
Pages 124-125: The Fnac store on Avenue des Ternes, Paris.

In September 1994, Artémis sold Fnac to the Pinault-Printemps-Redoute group. With revenue of 70.6 billion francs, the group became the European leader in consumer distribution and retail. It was the beginning of a new era.

A new dynamic

In February 1995, the Pinault-Printemps-Redoute group joined the CAC 40, the index listing the forty largest companies on the French stock market. This was a milestone event. In addition to recognizing the spectacular success of the company founded in 1962, which in the space of just a few years had become a European distribution and retail giant, it changed the situation in many respects. The group was now subject to new, very restrictive obligations in terms of financial communication and shareholder relations, and was more exposed to the scrutiny of the public, analysts, investors, and competitors. With its listing on the CAC 40, the group was at the beginning of a new dynamic.

To embody this fresh momentum, François Pinault chose Serge Weinberg, who had joined him in 1990 and had successively and successfully managed CFAO and then Rexel. In July 1995, Weinberg replaced Pierre Blayau as the chairman of the Pinault-Printemps-Redoute's Board. His strategy was clear: he wanted to accelerate the implementation of synergies and economies of scale, to intensify the share of international sales, to review and clarify the brands' positioning while ensuring that innovation was not left behind, with a particular focus on e-commerce. All these objectives would be met, and even exceeded, in less than five years.

The deals carried out simultaneously—and at great speed—immersed the group in perpetual movement that would profoundly change how it looked and how it operated. Immediately upon his arrival, Serge Weinberg expanded the action taken by his predecessor and began rethinking the group's organization with the aim of perfecting the coordination of its activities and encouraging initiative, entrepreneurship, and risk-taking. Those words had guided François Pinault from the beginning. "The group's growth fundamentally depends on the quality of its operations. We are in the service business: success depends on people. Those in charge all have one thing in common: they all have an entrepreneurial mindset. We have created an organization that allows them to take responsibility. Within the group, it must be possible to take risks. Such decentralization and the resulting empowerment must spread far and wide," explained Serge Weinberg in an interview with *L'Express* published shortly after his appointment.

For that reason, reversing the principle of decentralization, one of the group's key features, was out of the question. However, shared functions, multifunctional tools, shared procedures and possibilities for exchange would be instigated, to give form to the idea of the group, to homogenize its strategy, and to establish common objectives. To this end, an executive committee had been set up, bringing all the brands together for one day a month to exchange ideas and to manage shared actions in shared areas, such as marketing, basic resources, logistics, group purchasing, e-commerce, and so on. One of the objectives was to take advantage of each brand's database to improve marketing and customer efficiency. Another area of joint action was human resources. In 1995, a department of human resources and communications was created. Its mission was to establish a system of career planning, to encourage inter-brand mobility and to define shared recruitment standards. Through its participation in a number of student forums, the group worked to raise its profile with leading business schools—including HEC Paris, ESSEC, and ESCP—in order to attract young graduates who would go on to become the group's future senior executives.

"PPR depends on a balance between the impetus provided by the dissemination of responsibilities and the ability to work together," Serge Weinberg summarized in an interview with *Les Echos* in 1997, about the organization that had been put in place since 1995. "The goal was to avoid the group becoming locked into a hierarchy," he adds today. This balance between shared rationale and responsibility, which ensure flexibility and efficiency, remains one of the group's defining features. Of course, much of this is thanks to the diversity of the brands and companies that make up the group, each with its own history and culture, and each operating in different markets and business domains. But it also owes a great deal to the values that have guided the company since 1962, and to which it has remained faithful: an entrepreneurial spirit, responsiveness, a willingness to take risks, responsibility, and audacity, "which allows you to go where you're not expected, to build and to move forward," as François-Henri Pinault emphasizes today. These are the values that Serge Weinberg and his teams relied on to successfully grow the group.

Becoming international

Among the priorities defined by the new President of the Board on his arrival was of particular importance: becoming international. With the collapse of the USSR in 1991, the liberalization of global trade, the creation of the single European market in 1992, and the emergence of Asia as the "world's workshop," the early 1990s signaled the real beginning of globalization. The playing field for large French companies was no longer just France, but Europe, and even the entire world. That was where the market to be conquered would be found, along with market share and the drivers of growth. "Companies' appetite for international business has not diminished," noted the Crédit National in a 1993 study, emphasizing the continuous and sustained growth of physical investments made by French companies abroad since the start of the decade. In 1995, international investments represented 42 percent of total investment by French companies, compared to 31 percent in 1987. Every sector of activity was implicated, particularly distribution, both general and specialized. Driven by the emergence of a vast global middle class with increased purchasing power—one of the key features of the 1990s that would later have a major influence on the history of Kering—the company was opening an increasing number of stores around the world. It was the period when the large French retailer Carrefour opened its first hyper- and supermarkets in China, Italy, and Poland; its counterpart Casino moved into Latin America, and E. Leclerc established its presence in Spain and Eastern Europe. It was also the time when the Swedish chain Ikea really shifted scale: between 1990 and 1999, it opened some forty stores in Europe, the Middle East, and Asia, including thirteen in China.

For Serge Weinberg, the time had come for the group to take full advantage of the opportunities globalization offered. In 1995, the proportion

of Pinault-Printemps-Redoute's revenue generated outside France was a little less than 30 percent, similar to companies of comparable size. The goal was to increase the share to 40 percent in the year 2000. All of the group's sectors were involved in this momentum, to varying degrees. Starting with the professional distribution division, with Rexel undoubtedly the jewel in the crown. From 1995, the electrical distribution company, which already had a large network of sales points in Europe and North America, successively established itself in Brazil, Australia, New Zealand, and most of the Eastern European markets. In 1999, Rexel also consolidated its position in the United States by acquiring the Californian companies Norcal Electric Supply and Valley Electric Company. By that year, Rexel had become the world's leader in the distribution of electrical equipment, with a presence in thirty-three countries and more than 70 percent of its revenue generated outside France. Although Rexel was at the forefront, it was no longer the only member of the group with ambitions for professional distribution beyond France's borders. A decisive step forward came in 1998, with the acquisition of Guilbert, the leading European distributor of office supplies and furniture. Rexel and Guilbert, which had subsidiaries in Great Britain, Italy, Germany, Spain, and Belgium, now stood as twin pillars of the group's international professional distribution business. The timber business, the group's traditional domain, remained focused on France. Instead of conquering the world, the resources for which PPR was now reserving for its other businesses, Pinault Distribution was happy to consolidate its market share nationally. The 1997 acquisition of Becob, the company founded by André Lévy, father of philosopher Bernard-Henri Lévy, was another step in this direction. Dubbed Pinault Bois & Matériaux, the new entity created by the merging of the two companies strengthened its position as the leading distributor of timber and building materials in France, with 178 sales outlets.

But above everything else, it was the consumer retail division that experienced an accelerated global push, beginning in the mid-1990s. As a result, there was always much to do. In 1995, with the notable exception of La Redoute, the world's third-largest retailer, with a third of its sales generated outside France, the two brands with international potential, Conforama and Fnac, remained very French. The first had only two stores abroad, in Switzerland and Luxembourg, while the latter was only active in Brussels. Room for improvement was therefore quite considerable. However, their globalization was being vigorously pursued. Between 1996 and 1999, Conforama moved into Portugal, as well as Spain, where it took control of the hardware chain El Brico Hogar, which made it Spain's market leader in household appliances. In 1999, the brand entered markets in Asia, opening its first store in Taiwan. The same momentum could be seen with Fnac. As soon as he was appointed to lead the company in 1997, François-Henri Pinault made globalization one of his priorities. Under his command, the cultural products and leisure retailer established stores in Portugal, in Porto and Lisbon; and in Spain, in Barcelona and Valencia, before looking further afield. In 1997, the acquisition of the Atica Shopping Cultural chain provided it with a foothold in Brazil. Twelve months later, Fnac also opened a store in Taiwan.

At the same time, La Redoute consolidated its international positions. The mail-order company took a decisive step in 1998, taking control of the US mail-order company Brylane. With 10 million active clients and 1.4 billion euros in revenue, this company was clearly no giant in the sector but, in the highly fragmented American market, it represented for the group a valuable foundation, anticipating future developments. In addition, the company was distinctive for its catalog, which was revised fifty times a year, a unique approach in the sector. La Redoute also strengthened its European position by acquiring Ellos, the number one mail-order company in Scandinavia, which made it the sector's leader in Sweden, Norway, Denmark, Estonia, and Finland. In 1998, 25.5 percent of La Redoute's revenue was generated in Europe (excluding France) and 24.7 percent in the United States. Present in eighteen countries, it was the most international of all the brands within the group. One year later, to underline this mission, it took the name Redcats—"red" for La Redoute and "cats" for catalogs. This English-sounding name also helped unite a company with 23,000 employees, more than half of whom were outside France. The French brand of the mail order company, though, retained the name La Redoute.

In 1998, international business accounted for 44.2 percent of PPR's revenue. The group had far exceeded the targets it set in 1995. While Europe was still its main focus of activity (22 percent), it now had a solid foothold in the United States (14 percent) and had begun—with some caution—to position itself in Latin America and Asia. In this latter market, PPR created PPR Asia, a dedicated development organization based in Singapore. Its mission was to identify development opportunities as well as local partners, especially in the consumer retail sector. The group had worked with a local partner in Taiwan, President Enterprises, to open its Fnac store. Like François Pinault, Serge Weinberg was convinced that there was formidable potential in Asia for growing its consumer retail activities. Major specialized brands were already established there, including Ikea, which opened a store in Taiwan in 1994, and was readying itself to enter Mainland China in 1998. Through PPR Asia, the group studied a number of projects in Thailand, the Philippines, Indonesia, and China. They finally did not come to fruition because of the financial crisis that hit that part of the world in 1997 and 1998. Ultimately, it would only be when the group launched into the world of luxury that the Asian markets would really come into their full importance.

Innovation

Internationalizing PPR's consumer retail brands was not its only strategy to fulfill its stated ambition: to establish itself as one of the world's leading players in specialized retailing and services. The ongoing enhancement of the group's offering, the launch of new activities, and the development of new concepts and product lines were also having a significant effect. Printemps is a good case in point. Starting in 1996, the department store on Boulevard Haussmann, which welcomed 60,000 visitors per day, was the object of considerable investment. The goal was to modernize its image while expanding the range of its offer. Women's fashion, beauty, and accessories were completely redesigned to include products corresponding to the major trends of the time, and those likely to appeal to the "modern woman," as an advertisement of the time emphasized. At the same time, a new space dedicated to leisure was created. For their part, the Prisunic stores adopted a new strategic position, catering to urban women.

In order to not be left behind, other brands were exploring original concepts. Fnac, for example, launched Fnac Junior in 1997, while in 1998, Conforama opened a store in Boulogne-Billancourt devoted to the world of the kitchen and cooking. With regard to consumer retailing, the

Pinault-Printemps-Redoute group was also developing in new directions, including sport, with the creation of the chain of Made in Sport stores, aimed at fifteen- to twenty-five-year-olds, and women's lingerie, with the new brand Orcanta. On the other hand, in 1997, the group entered a new, very unexpected market: telecommunications. That year, Pinault-Printemps-Redoute launched a new telecommunications operator for the general public. Its name, Kertel, was coined from the words "ker"—"home" in Breton—and telecommunications. Though the group was not the first alternative operator to launch in France—it was notably preceded by Bouygues Telecom and Cegetel—it stood apart for its positioning. The idea was to capitalize on its distribution experience and to use partnerships to establish itself as the preferred operator for distribution companies in all sectors. As soon as it was launched, Kertel signed agreements with Casino, Continent, Carrefour, Shell, Relais H, and of course, with Redcats, Printemps, Fnac, and Conforama. The operator offered rechargeable prepaid cards to these brands. By the end of 1998, it had already distributed more than 400,000. Kertel could now turn to the residential telecommunications market, which it did in 1999 with Kerbox, a router capable of not only automatically recognizing the number dialed, but of offering the subscriber the best rate, a genuine innovation in the world of telecommunications.

With Kertel, the group demonstrated its interest in creating new companies—a strong part of its history since 1962—and in technological innovation. This interest was also reflected in its early moves into e-commerce. As early as 1995, La Redoute, which had previously distributed its catalogs on digital disks (CD-ROMS), launched its first French-language e-commerce website. PPR was clearly a pioneer: at that time there were less than two hundred e-commerce sites in the world, all in the United States. The most promising of them, Amazon, was launched just a few weeks earlier, in July 1995; eBay, another superstar in online selling, was inaugurated on September 3, 1995. In France, there was no comparable site. This was no surprise, since only 1.8 million French people had a computer, and of these, only 58,000 were connected to the World Wide Web. The country was still loyal to the Minitel, which had appeared in the early 1980s: it combined telephony and computing to access a variety of services, including those of both La Redoute and Fnac. But that French invention was only available on the national network and offered a limited number of functions.

In September 1995, La Redoute opened what was arguably the first French e-commerce site. In doing this, Pinault-Printemps-Redoute made its presence felt and positioned itself within a distribution method that no one doubted would revolutionize, in a very short timeframe, the world of commerce. From 1996–97, online commerce would, in fact, spread throughout France and the world. Fnac took the plunge in 1997. And it was in the United States that the company's director, François-Henri Pinault, found the inspiration. "My arrival at Fnac coincided with the emergence of digital. Being young, I was very comfortable in this new universe, which was not the case for most of Fnac's managers. With Fnac, the growth of digital was natural. At the time, there was Fnac 3615, which enabled us to make some sales remotely. In 1997, I took my teams to Palo Alto, California, which was the world laboratory for the digital economy. That's when we set up the Fnac.com site," he explains. Some 400,000 cultural and leisure products—books, disks, videos, and CD-ROMS—were available. Shortly after its launch, it was one of the most visited e-commerce sites in France, with almost 2 million unique visitors. Internal initiatives then mushroomed. Between 1997 and 1999, all of PPR's consumer and professional brands developed their own e-commerce sites in France, Europe, and the United States. On the other side of the Atlantic, the group took a major step in 1999, acquiring control of Mobile Planet, an American leader in the online sales of computer products.

Following this deal, Pinault-Printemps-Redoute had a total of forty-five e-commerce sites, making it the World Wide Web's most active specialized retailer. A comprehensive online strategy was being deployed across the group. In April 2000, it reached a milestone, with the appointment of François-Henri Pinault as Deputy CEO in charge of e-commerce. His objectives were to integrate the Internet into all the group's businesses and to build a click-and-mortar strategy combining traditional distribution channels, i.e. stores, and digital tools. At the dawn of the 2000s, the group had already mastered the technological challenges of online sales. His experience would prove incredibly beneficial in the future.

Readying for battle

In 1999, on the eve of the major maneuvers that would see the group make a totally unexpected foray into the world of luxury, its revenue reached 124 billion francs (the equivalent of 18.9 billion euros) and employed 90,000 people around the world. With 48 percent of this revenue generated outside France—the 50 percent mark would be passed in 2000—PPR had become a truly international group. It was organized into three major growth areas: consumer retail (52 percent of revenue), professional distribution (42 percent), and international sales, with CFAO (6 percent). The group had not made any other significant divestments, apart from selling the Prisunic chain to Monoprix in 1997.

After five years of accelerated growth, the group was profoundly changed. More international, more diversified, it was also much more efficient. All its business lines, purchasing costs, logistics, and the circulation of information had been optimized in order to improve operating methods with suppliers and expediate stock rotation. In 1996, PPR established a purchasing office in Hong Kong for its mail order company Redcats. "The goal was to cut out local middlemen and create direct relationships with suppliers. That office allowed us a complete overview of the production chain, so we could verify that the finished product's quality met our requirements and we set up a tracking system. It was also tasked with identifying new suppliers able to operate across the group, while each company retained a great deal of freedom in terms of purchasing. This was an innovative approach in the retail sector. At the time, only a handful of large central offices had this type of organization," explains Françoise Devé, who opened the purchasing office. In addition, it was characteristic of PPR's determination to utilize shared tools without ignoring the principle of decentralization. It was also in line with the long tradition that François Pinault had inaugurated in 1965: to do without intermediaries wherever possible.

Beyond anything else, within the space of five years the group had increased the speed of its cultural transformation. The very rapid rise of mass-market retailing, the creation of new store concepts dedicated to certain kinds of products geared toward clearly identified segments of the population—juniors, fifteen- to twenty-five-year-olds, working women, and so on—and developments in e-commerce had given PPR brand culture and a deep understanding of its products and consumer expectations. It had become a client specialist. Thanks to its decentralized organization around leading companies, strong brands, and a variety of different kinds of stores, it was able to continually anticipate and satisfy customer expectations. To better meet these expectations, the group had developed new services and acquired new skills, particularly in the fields of advertising and marketing. Through its retail operations, especially Printemps, Pinault-Printemps-Redoute was also becoming familiar with the world of luxury. "The group was gradually moving from the tangible to the intangible with an increasing focus on the brand," Jean-François Palus explains today. This shift picked up pace with the acquisition of a stake in Gucci.

LUXURY, THE NEW EL DORADO

On March 19, 1999, Pinault-Printemps-Redoute announced that it had simultaneously acquired a 42 percent stake in Gucci and 100 percent of Yves Saint Laurent. The group's dramatic entry into the luxury market took everyone by surprise. And although it was not part of a premeditated strategy, it is not quite as surprising as it may have seemed.

An unexpected move into the world of luxury

Everything began in February 1999. In Paris, François Pinault met with the American investment banker Joseph Perella, a financial adviser to Gucci, the prestigious Italian luxury brand founded in 1921. The American banker explained to the French entrepreneur that the businessman Domenico De Sole, with the support of the young American designer Tom Ford, had been striving to turn the brand around since 1994, but that it was gradually coming under the control of LVMH, the luxury group founded by Bernard Arnault. To understand the situation and the importance of Gucci for PPR, a brief review of its history is in order.

The story starts in 1921 when Guccio Gucci, on his return from London, where he had been working as a bellhop at the Savoy, opened a small boutique in Florence selling leather goods and luggage to passing tourists. Guccio Gucci, with his impeccable aesthetic, designed his creations around the English aristocracy's taste for horseback riding, which he came to understand during his stay in Britain, and by taking advantage of the possibilities offered by Florence's renowned leathercraft. The young entrepreneur not only found buyers in Italy, but in England, Germany, and France, meaning he was able to simultaneously build a discerning international clientele. During the Roaring Twenties, when the rich spent lavishly, such high-end positioning brought success to the small company.

In the early 1930s, Guccio Gucci began making his own pieces in a workshop located behind his Florentine store. A few years later, in 1938, he opened a second store in Rome. The Gucci brand was taking off. It was also in the 1930s, in 1933 to be precise, that the House's soon-to-be-iconic logo, with its two intertwined Gs, was born. Paradoxically, it was wartime shortages that ultimately established the logo. From 1940, without raw materials, Guccio Gucci used linen or bamboo for certain elements, in lieu of leather. Launched in 1947, the famous bamboo bag was a major part of the brand's success.

Guccio Gucci died in 1953, leaving his legacy to his four sons. The 1960s were marked by significant developments. The House's bags were coveted by the world's celebrities, from Jackie Kennedy, who even lent her name to the *Jackie* bag, to Samuel Beckett and Princess Grace of Monaco, who commissioned a scarf called *Flora*. Gucci gradually expanded its retail network to the United States and Asia. A victim of family quarrels between the Gucci brothers, the brand experienced a sudden decline in the 1980s. In 1987, Maurizio Gucci, one of the founder's grandsons, unable to reverse the company's fortunes, sold it to Investcorp, an investment company from the United Arab Emirates, which listed it on the New York Stock Exchange. Appointed CEO in 1994, Domenico De Sole set to work reviving the company, with the help of Ford. With inspiration and vision, the latter thoroughly renewed the brand's codes. Breaking from the classical style, he focused on luxurious, sensual minimalism. At the same time, Domenico

Left: Guccio Gucci, the House's founder, c. 1940.
Right: Roberto Gucci, one of the founder's grandsons,
talking to a craftsman at one of the House's workshops.

De Sole modernized the company's organization and operating methods. Particular attention was paid to artisanal production, to ensure quality. As was the case during Guccio Gucci's time, production was once again carried out in the Florentine workshops, relying on traditional Tuscan expertise. The brand also increased the number of stores opening around the world. Under the leadership of Domenico De Sole and Tom Ford, the Italian brand had become one of the luxury sector's major players. It was at this moment that Bernard Arnault, CEO of LVMH, decided to acquire a share of its capital.

At the beginning of January 1999, he acquired 5 percent of the Florentine leather goods manufacturer and he continued increasing his stake in the company. By February, he controlled 34.4 percent, and everything seemed to suggest that he would not stop there. Domenico De Sole was determined to block LVMH from taking over Gucci. After devising several schemes to dilute the luxury giant's share, he decided to bring in a new investor, a "white knight." This was when he thought of François Pinault. Hence, Joseph Perella's visit to Paris in February 1999. For the Italian businessman, François Pinault had two substantial advantages: first, he was not from the luxury world but from that of retail, so would not be tempted to take control of Gucci; and second, he had the financial resources to go head-to-head with Bernard Arnault if needed.

François Pinault was immediately interested. His decision was not the consequence of long, strategic reflection, although Serge Weinberg had been considering acquiring a major brand for some time. In this instance, as he had done so often in the past, the entrepreneur acted intuitively, seizing the opportunity when it presented itself. And what better opportunity than to become the largest shareholder in one of the world's most prestigious luxury houses? François Pinault did not, however, make the decision on a whim. It was based on a number of strong insights and a precise analysis of PPR's limits, the environment it was operating in, and the avenues available for growth. "To embrace globalization and take full advantage of it, we had to have global brands that were instantly recognizable across the world," he explains today. In brief, to change scale PPR had to invest directly in brands with strong global recognition, rather than concentrating on retail and distribution and developing localized brands.

The change was all the more welcome because the global retail landscape was transforming rapidly. In the food sector, the trend toward consolidation and globalization was accelerating. For example, French-style hypermarkets were established all over the world, Carrefour and Promodès merged, and the American company Walmart moved into the European market. In 1999, the world's five leading retailers—Walmart, Carrefour, Ahold, Tesco, and Auchan—recorded revenue of 400 billion euros, twice that of 1995. The same trend could be seen in textiles with brands such as Zara and H&M, which were expanding far beyond their home markets, acquiring recognition comparable to that of Coca-Cola or McDonald's. Ultimately, e-commerce was changing the landscape, expanding the market to new operators, and literally breaking down national boundaries. In this climate, the transformation of PPR into a global retail group was going to require considerable time and investment. A challenge that Jean-François Palus sums up well: "A retail concept can only spread in concentric circles, and only gradually. On the other hand, a brand, which is completely intangible, can be immediately projected far from the country in which it was born or its environment. Its potential is instantaneously global."

For François Pinault, the decision to acquire Gucci's capital was connected to ideas of how PPR could rapidly establish itself, in the best conditions, as a truly global group. At the same time, he realized something: across the globe, the only genuinely identifiable brands were from the world of sport and, even more, the world of luxury. An astute observer, the entrepreneur had taken on board the changes of the previous decade. The globalization that had begun in the early 1990s had brought the luxury industry into a new era. The opening up of markets, the emergence of a vast global middle class and its accompanying purchasing power, the homogenization of behaviors, and the spread of new values built around the individual offered immense growth opportunities, especially in Asia. Indeed Asia, and China in particular, had become the luxury paradise that it would be when Millennials, the generation born in the 1980s and 1990s, began buying prestigious brands on a massive scale. That time would arrive soon enough, at the beginning of the third millennium. In the early 2000s, Chinese clients still represented only 1 percent of the world's luxury purchases; by 2018, that figure would be 33 percent. For the sector's major brands, Asia was already an important market. Most were already established there, sometimes for a long time, including Cartier, Hermès, Christian Dior, Chanel, and Louis Vuitton, not to mention Ralph Lauren, Calvin Klein, Armani, and Versace.

At the end of the 1990s, the global luxury market was booming. In just ten years, its revenue had gone from 44.5 to almost 90 billion euros. In 2007, it reached 190 billion euros and, in 2021, 283 billion. With an annual growth rate of 6 to 8 percent, the sector was thriving, flourishing in fact. With the high level of investment required to establish global distribution networks, in the 1990s the sector already was quite concentrated. In 1999, when PPR was readying its entrance, the luxury market was made up of a few powerful stakeholders, some of which were listed on the stock exchange and had significant resources, such as LVMH, Richemont, Chanel, and Hermès, and a number of small- and medium-sized companies, often still family-owned. The largest groups controlled more than eighty internationally renowned luxury brands. If exclusive brands belonging to leaders in the hygiene and beauty sector are added — among them L'Oréal, Estée Lauder, and Coty — large groups own almost 130 brands and control a combined 65 percent of the world's luxury brands.

It was the chance for PPR to fully participate in the major wave of globalization and "benefit from the growth of international trade," to borrow Serge Weinberg's expression; to access an expanding market, particularly in Asia, and many growth opportunities, not to mention much higher profitability than in distribution. These were the reasons behind François Pinault's decision to seize the opportunity Domenico De Sole offered him and take a stake in Gucci. In addition, luxury goods were not entirely foreign to PPR. It was aligned with the group's activities, which at the time generated 22 percent of its revenue through apparel and personal goods. Moreover, physical retail stores are key elements in the luxury business.

Domenico De Sole and François Pinault met in London in early March 1999 to work out the final details of their coalition. At this meeting, the Italian businessman suggested to the French entrepreneur that he establish Gucci as the foundation of a luxury group that could rival the sector's two global leaders, LVMH and Richemont. And this was effectively the plan chosen. It was then the turn of the teams to get involved. Throughout March, the staff of the future partners met in the British capital, in utmost secrecy, to define the deal's technical aspects. This would take the form of a reserved capital increase. Implementing the 3 billion dollars in financing and the legal aspects were completed within forty-eight hours.

On March 19, 1999, the announcement of PPR's entry into the history of Gucci with a 42 percent stake surprised investors. The latter had been expecting a large outside acquisition in retail and distribution, and Serge Weinberg was in fact also interested in the assets of British group Kingfisher, especially But, Castorama, and Darty. Yet again, François Pinault took everyone by surprise. That deal wasn't all: on the same day, he announced that through Artémis, he had acquired Sanofi Beauté, a branch of the French pharmaceutical group Sanofi, for 910 million euros, including the brands Yves Saint Laurent and Roger & Gallet, and the license for Van Cleef & Arpels fragrances. PPR's dramatic entry into the world of luxury not only surprised all those following the group but also its employees, for whom the news was, as the press wrote, "like a thunderclap in a clear sky," and, of course, LVMH, which had not seen it coming and which was preparing its own takeover bid for the Italian brand. Thus, it also marked the beginning of a long legal battle between PPR and Bernard Arnault, which held a 20.6 percent stake in the Florentine leather goods maker, with LVMH contesting the terms of the reserved capital increase that Gucci launched for PPR. LVMH tried to prove that the agreement signed between PPR and the two directors of the luxury House benefited only the financial interests of the latter and not those of the company. At the center of its argument: the notion that the stock options that Tom Ford and Domenico De Sole were to receive, valued at 800 million US dollars, a considerable sum considering Gucci's size, were negotiated in advance to persuade them to prefer PPR's offer. The two men obviously disputed this interpretation: according to them, the stock options were granted after and not before the agreement.

It was only on September 10, 2001, after several legal challenges and under the aegis of Alain Minc and Belgian businessman Albert Frère, that an agreement was finally reached between Bernard Arnault and François Pinault, who initially undertook to acquire 8.6 percent of the shares owned by LVMH, then to buy back 100 percent of Gucci's shares by March 2004. Pinault-Printemps-Redoute, which believed it could control the luxury brand with a stake of just over 44 percent, would thus pay a further 8.6 billion dollars in less than three years. The agreement also included specific clauses initially planned between François Pinault, Domenico De Sole, and Tom Ford: PPR would not have a voice in Gucci's strategic direction before March 2004, and the Italian company would have the right to review any planned acquisition by the group in the luxury sector. In other words, until 2004, the PPR group would finance Gucci's growth without being able to position itself in place of the management team formed by Domenico De Sole and Tom Ford.

On September 10, 2001, many observers were curious about how much maneuverability PPR would find at Gucci and, more than anything else, the group's ability to finalize its takeover bid for the Italian flagship in 2004. All the more so after September 11, 2001, just one day after the agreement was made public. The September 11 attacks plunged the world economy, and in particular the luxury goods industry, into an era of doubt and instability. The price of PPR shares fell sharply, reflecting the financial community's concerns. While most of François Pinault's advisers and collaborators suggested that he use the clause covering exceptional circumstances to revisit the terms of the agreement signed with LVMH, he refused to compromise. He would not give in. He could see clearly where he was going. Although the Gucci acquisition cost him more than expected, it also gave him the chance to become a global player in the luxury goods sector, thus ushering in another shift in his activities. In fact, as soon as the deal was finalized, the group began working on growing its new Luxury division.

Steadily building a Luxury division

"Our ambition is to create a large group around Gucci that brings together our other brands. Luxury goods will very rapidly represent a relatively significant part of our business." In the wake of securing a stake in Gucci and the takeover of Sanofi Beauté, the group, through Serge Weinberg, stated its ambitions loudly and clearly: indeed, it was a question of creating a large multi-brand division dedicated to luxury alongside the divisions that already existed. Within the group, the new activity was still very marginal at this stage, accounting for only 4 percent of revenue. But it was supported by two leading brands, Gucci and Yves Saint Laurent. With revenue of just over 1 billion dollars, 41 percent of which was in leather goods, Gucci was a genuinely global brand. It was present in the United States, Asia, and Europe, and had 131 of its own stores. Yves Saint Laurent, which included Yves Saint Laurent Beauté and Yves Saint Laurent Couture, operated fifteen stores in Europe, the United States, Japan, and Hong Kong. These are the brands around which PPR would begin to build its Luxury division.

In 1999, as already decided, François Pinault transferred Yves Saint Laurent's capital to Gucci, creating the Gucci Group, the world's third-largest luxury goods company, behind LVMH and Richemont. Domenico De Sole and Tom Ford immediately applied the formulas that had made Gucci a success to the French brand: the discontinuation of licenses, the expansion of product lines—particularly accessories—and the opening of new directly-owned stores. Synergies between the two brands were also put into place. For example, Yves Saint Laurent's watch straps and other leather accessories were manufactured by Gucci's workshops. Above all, the Gucci Group increased its acquisitions. While Domenico De Sole and Tom Ford were at the helm, the industrial project underpinning such external growth was defined in close consultation with the Pinault-Printemps-Redoute group. A five-person strategic and financial committee was established within the Gucci Group, including three members appointed by PPR, to advise management on strategic acquisitions. The group also earmarked significant resources of 4 to 5 billion euros, to carry out "selective purchases of longstanding brands with strong growth potential."

The first step came in 1999, with the takeover of Sergio Rossi, the Italian luxury women's footwear brand founded in 1951. The following year, the Gucci Group acquired the jewelry and watchmaking House Boucheron, whose history dates back to 1858 and which has always been housed in the Hôtel de Nocé mansion on Place Vendôme in Paris. Things started moving even faster in 2001. That year, the Gucci Group made several pivotal acquisitions that would prove decisive in for the future. It first took control of Bottega Veneta, the luxury leather goods brand founded in Milan in 1966, manufacturer of the famous *intrecciato* bags. The new group then acquired the fashion House Balenciaga, founded in 1917 by Spanish designer Cristóbal Balenciaga and established in Paris since 1936. With Nicolas Ghesquière, Artistic Director since 1997, the brand was experiencing a renaissance. The Gucci

Left: Serge Weinberg, François Pinault, Tom Ford, and Domenico De Sole in 1999.
Right: François Pinault and Yves Saint Laurent in 2000.

Group also acquired stakes in two emerging eponymous brands helmed by talented young English fashion designers: Alexander McQueen, and Stella McCartney, a joint venture between the Gucci Group and the brand namesake designer, a daughter of Paul McCartney. Stella McCartney was one of the first in the fashion world to find alternatives to leather and to use 100 percent natural materials, including organic cotton and bamboo fiber. It was taking the group on a path that had not yet been explored by anyone else in the sector.

In 2002, following the first wave of acquisitions, the revenue generated by PPR's Luxury division reached 2.5 billion euros, or just over 9 percent of the group as a whole. It now had eight brands: Gucci, Yves Saint Laurent, Sergio Rossi, Boucheron, Bottega Veneta, Alexander McQueen, Stella McCartney, and Balenciaga. The presence of well-known, sometimes historical, houses alongside young or developing brands, on which the group had not hesitated to gamble, was one of the characteristics of PPR. And this remains true today. The group was designing, producing, and distributing an enormous range of luxury products: leather goods, luggage, handbags, scarves, ready-to-wear, shoes, jewelry, watches, glasses, fragrances, and more. Extremely profitable, with a 12.1 percent operating margin as opposed to 5.1 percent for consumer and professional retail and distribution, this division was also truly international. It generated 30.7 percent of its revenue in Europe, 24 percent in the United States, 25 percent in Japan, and 17 percent in the rest of Asia, especially in Hong Kong and Mainland China.

Under the leadership of Domenico De Sole, priority was given to controlling distribution. This strategy was indispensable in ensuring coherence in the identity of each brand across the Gucci Group. While traditional luxury retailing had happened through directly-operated, franchise, duty-free, department, and specialty stores, a major effort was now focusing on developing the directly-operated network as a priority. New Gucci, Yves Saint Laurent, and Sergio Rossi stores opened in prestigious locations, including Avenue Montaigne in Paris, Madison Avenue in New York, Bond Street in London, and Via Monte Napoleone in Milan. In 2002, the ensemble of luxury brands constituting the Gucci Group operated 336 of their own stores, including 173 for Gucci and 46 for Yves Saint Laurent. The Gucci Group had also successfully increased the number of collaborations between its brands, employing Gucci's leather goods craftsmanship, Sergio Rossi's knowledge of shoes, and Yves Saint Laurent Beauté's expertise in fragrances and cosmetics. Though each brand managed its own product and store design, a number of functions had been pooled, particularly concerning logistics and IT.

Overall, it took just four years for Pinault-Printemps-Redoute to begin building its Luxury division. Compared to the giants in the sector, though, the group remained modest. Moreover, not all brands were progressing at the same rate. Yves Saint Laurent had been losing momentum for some time and required major investment. Despite the economic recession that had hit the world since the Internet bubble burst in 2000 and the September 11 attacks in 2001, the sector's growth prospects remained extremely promising. To the point of considering transforming luxury goods into one of Pinault-Printemps-Redoute's main business activities. Within the group, there were plans to refocus PPR on two areas: luxury and consumer distribution. Those two ecosystems are in fact eminently complementary in terms of clientele and distribution channels. In such a configuration, the group's other business, most notably professional distribution, would lose strategic significance.

Portrait of Frédéric Boucheron, founder of the high jewelry House.

Alexander McQueen in 2005, wearing a sneaker
developed in collaboration with Puma.

Cristóbal Balenciaga in 1927.

Villa Schroeder-Da Porto in Venetia, Italy,
Bottega Veneta's headquarters and workshops since 2013.

This refocusing, filled with future challenges, was initiated in 2002. That year, PPR sold Guilbert, its remote office supplies company, to the American company Staples, and its financial services division in France and Scandinavia to Crédit Agricole and BNP Paribas. Developed by the group at the time it entered consumer distribution and retailing, the credit and financial services division included a number of jewels, among them Finaref. Initially centered on credit, with cards, personal loans, and insurance, it quickly moved into savings. In 2001, Finaref created the Finaref-ABN Amro savings bank. The profitable division's revenue had been constantly growing. As part of its new strategy, however, PPR decided to sell the company to finance new developments. That same year, 2002, the group increased its stake in Gucci to 54.4 percent. This marked the beginning of a new strategic transformation, which would begin to be fully implemented in 2003.

HOPITAL LAENNEC
La Cour d'honneur

Laennec

"Deciding to establish ourselves here is a reflection of our Parisian and French roots. We now have a home of our own. In its singularity and boldness, this place resembles us. It is a place for a different kind of luxury, free to make its own choices."

FRANÇOIS-HENRI PINAULT

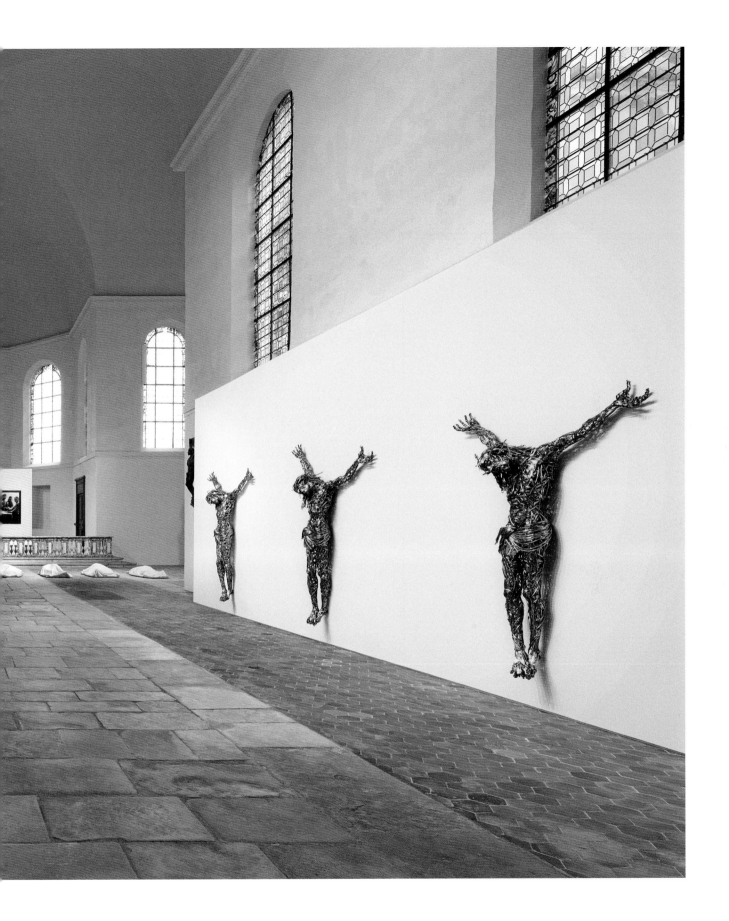

A GLOBAL LUXURY GIANT

The year 2003 opened a new chapter in the group's history. That year, in the culmination of a process that had begun in 2001, François-Henri Pinault succeeded François Pinault at the head of Artémis, the holding company of the Pinault-Printemps-Redoute group; two years later, he took over the group's operational management. This marked the beginning of a major strategic shift. In the space of a few years, the company had refocused on Luxury and Sport & Lifestyle, while divesting itself of its professional and consumer distribution activities by stages. Renamed Kering in 2013, the group completed its transformation by becoming a pure player in luxury from 2018. Now one of the industry's world leaders, Kering stands apart for its vision of creative luxury and its commitment to sustainable luxury.

François-Henri Pinault and François Pinault at Laennec, the Kering headquarters,
during an exhibition of contemporary artwork from the Pinault Collection,
organized as part of European Heritage Days in 2018.

A MAJOR STRATEGIC SHIFT

In May 2003, François and François-Henri Pinault met for a very special dinner at L'Ami Louis, a restaurant in the 3rd arrondissement of Paris. It was here that the entrepreneur told his son that he was entrusting him with the reins of Artémis, the family holding company that controls the Pinault-Printemps-Redoute group. This orderly succession had been prepared for quite some time.

Passing the baton

The first step had been taken in 2001, when François-Henri Pinault became, alongside his father, Co-Manager and Director of Financière Pinault, the umbrella holding company of Artémis. At almost forty, François-Henri was already able to look back on a rich career within the family group. Since 1987 he had undertaken a true "initiatory journey"—as the newspaper *Le Monde* described it—which began in a sawmill and continued in an office of Pinault France, before leading him to successively head CFAO and Fnac, and then finally to the Deputy General Management of Pinault-Printemps-Redoute, where he oversaw e-commerce. His successes in all these varied roles, especially with Fnac, helped establish his legitimacy. "Fnac is a very large company. My experience at its head was important in my personal journey. It also meant a lot to my father. I think it is what made him decide on me as his successor," he says today. In fact, through his involvement in Financière Pinault and Artémis, and his engagement in the group's major strategic decisions, François-Henri Pinault was clearly positioned as the natural successor to François Pinault.

In May 2003, Pinault Sr. decided to entrust his son with the presidency of Artémis, believing that he had the necessary skills to succeed him. "He was ready and I didn't see the need to wait any longer," the entrepreneur told *Paris Match* magazine in October 2013. That evening at the restaurant L'Ami Louis, François Pinault symbolically embodied the transfer of power by giving François-Henri a key ring with the key to his office at Artémis. "I gave it to him and said: 'Next Monday, you're moving into my office. You're forty-one years old. It's your turn!'" he continued. An atypical handover, to say the least, "elegant and efficient," as François-Henri Pinault says today. His appointment as head of Artémis became effective on May 15, 2003. Although François Pinault's withdrawal was genuine, it did not mean he had lost interest in the group's future. Quite the contrary. The filial relationship would remain constant, with the son regularly seeking the father's advice. "I will continue to use and take advantage of his advice. I know that during the difficult decisions that I will surely have to make, I will be able to rely on his counsel and his experience," declared François-Henri Pinault in an interview with *Les Echos* on the day he took up his position.

In the history of the group's governance, 2003 was an important first step. Another would follow in 2005. For the time being, with the support of Serge Weinberg and his teams, François-Henri Pinault continued working on the group's transformation.

Toward a new model

As soon as he took over as head of Artémis in May 2003, François-Henri Pinault decided to finalize and accelerate the refocus on the two complementary businesses of retail and luxury, a strategy initiated in 2002 with the sale of Guilbert and the credit and financial services division in France and Scandinavia. At that time, consumer retail represented 44.1 percent of the group's total revenue. It brought together the Printemps, Fnac, Conforama, and Redcats groups (which included the La Redoute, Verbaudet, and Cyrillus brands, among others, as well as Ellos in Scandinavia and an American branch). Luxury goods, as mentioned, accounted for just under 10 percent of the group's activity. Along with these unequally balanced divisions, professional distribution and financial services still accounted for 43.7 percent, respectively, and a little less than 3 percent of Pinault-Printemps-Redoute's total revenue. By deciding to withdraw from these two sectors, the group was preparing to redefine its structure completely.

In May 2003, Pinault-Printemps-Redoute sold Pinault Bois & Matériaux (1.3 billion euros in revenue)—then France's second largest distributor of building materials and timber imports/processing—to the British group Wolseley, the world leader in the distribution of heating and plumbing products and one of the leading distributors of building materials in the British and American markets. With this deal, a significant page in the group's history was turned. It was in the timber trade that François Pinault had begun his astonishing entrepreneurial adventure in 1962. While this deal was being made, the group continued its withdrawal from financial services by selling its remaining interests in Finaref and its subsidiary Facet to Crédit Agricole and BNP Paribas. The following year, in 2004, Rexel, which dominated the global distribution of electrical equipment with revenue of 6.8 billion euros and a presence in thirty countries, was sold to a consortium of investment funds. This was another milestone, because Rexel, which François Pinault and Serge Weinberg had transformed from a major French SME into a global giant, embodied the entrepreneurial spirit of the group and its founder. In just two years, Pinault-Printemps-Redoute had almost completely withdrawn from professional distribution and financial services. At that time, retail accounted for 60 percent of revenue and luxury just over 13 percent.

Luxury was the group's other strategic priority. Since 2002, the Gucci Group had continued to grow steadily, with the opening of more than twenty new Gucci, Yves Saint Laurent, and Sergio Rossi stores. In the immediate future, however, the main issue would remain control of the company, which Pinault-Printemps-Redoute was slated to acquire in full by March 2004, according to the terms of the contract signed on September 10, 2001. In 2002, as mentioned, the group already owned just over 54 percent of the company. A new level was reached in September 2003, with the group increasing its stake to 67.6 percent. It was now ready to launch a takeover bid on the balance of the capital. However, there was still one problem to be solved: the situation of Domenico De Sole and Tom Ford. Over time, relations between the two men and the management of Pinault-Printemps-Redoute had deteriorated. Tensions came from the delay in Yves Saint Laurent's recovery but also, above all, from the autonomy demanded by De Sole and Ford from a majority shareholder determined to regain control of its Luxury division. These issues came to an end in November 2003, when the group announced that it was parting ways with the two Gucci executives, with their departure effective in April 2004. To replace De Sole, François-Henri Pinault and Serge Weinberg turned to someone quite unexpected, the Dutch executive Robert Polet, formerly of Unilever. The announcement of his arrival at the head of the world's number three luxury goods company—he would take office on July 1—was like a thunderclap across every sector. It was explained in terms of needing to improve the still fragile profitability of Pinault-Printemps-Redoute's Luxury division. As for Gucci's artistic direction, it was first entrusted to a trio: Alessandra Facchinetti, John Ray, and Frida Giannini. Stefano Pilati was handed the creative reins of Yves Saint Laurent.

On March 22, 2004, the group announced the launch of its take-over bid for Gucci. By its completion in May, Pinault-Printemps-Redoute would hold 99.4 percent of the luxury group's capital. It was now free to implement expansion.

A "new PPR"

After the 2003 milestone in the evolution of the group's governance, another was reached in 2005. That year, François-Henri Pinault succeeded Serge Weinberg at the head of Pinault-Printemps-Redoute. It had been nearly two years since François-Henri Pinault had taken over from his father as head of Artémis, and so once again, it was no great surprise that he was preparing to assume management of the group. "I wanted to go beyond the presidency of Artémis, to take on operational leadership. So as early as 2003, alongside Serge Weinberg, I prepared to move to the head of the group," says François-Henri Pinault. Acting in concert, things went smoothly, especially as Serge Weinberg, after a decade at the helm of Pinault-Printemps-Redoute, wanted to pursue new entrepreneurial adventures. The handover took place in February 2005, when François-Henri Pinault officially became Chairman of the Board of Pinault-Printemps-Redoute.

His arrival at the group's head was accompanied by major transformations. First, there were changes to the executive team. These included naming Jean-François Palus as Financial Director of Artémis; Christophe Cuvillier as the head of Conforama; Thierry Guibert as the group's Financial Control Director, before moving to the financial department of Fnac; and Valérie Hermann as President of Yves Saint Laurent. Many of the new team that François-Henri Pinault put together were, like him, graduates of HEC Paris. Next came strategic changes. In February 2005, Serge Weinberg's successor launched a comprehensive audit with the objectives of reducing Pinault-Printemps-Redoute's operating costs and clarifying its strategic positioning. The reports made at the time were clearly an extension of those that resulted in François Pinault entering the world of luxury in 1999. "In 2005, Europe accounted for more than 70 percent of revenue, with nearly 25 percent of that in France alone. This dependence on the Old Continent represented a real risk for Pinault-Printemps-Redoute. That's when we decided to resolutely refocus on luxury, the most international of the group's activities, and the one with the strongest growth prospects. This meant phasing out consumer retailing and distribution, which was difficult to rapidly project into most dynamic emerging markets, except by engaging in large-scale acquisitions. In addition to the possibility of quickly penetrating these markets, luxury had another advantage: the power of its brands meant barriers to entry were high," says François-Henri Pinault.

In 2005, in deciding to focus on luxury, but also more broadly, as we will see, on major "personal equipment" brands, the group's intention was to accelerate and intensify the strategic transformation launched six years earlier when it acquired a stake in Gucci. The goal was to firmly position itself in the sector that was experiencing the strongest growth dynamic on a global scale. Indeed, after the slowdown of the early 2000s, luxury had returned to high growth rates, averaging 7 percent between 2004 and 2005. Asia was once again leading the way, with luxury sales growing by nearly 17 percent year-on-year. In that part of the world, China was the most promising market. Sales there had increased by 20 percent, significantly more than in Japan (+16 percent). They now exceeded 2 billion US dollars, making the country the third-largest market in the world, behind Europe and the United States. The Chinese market offered many advantages: a gross domestic product growth of more than 9 percent, an already large number of dollar millionaires—300,000 according to a Merrill Lynch study published in 2005—and a booming middle class. According to the report, the number of Chinese with an income in excess of 30,000 US dollars—the equivalent of 140,000 dollars in American terms—was then between five and ten million and growing rapidly. The immense Chinese market had another advantage for luxury players: the wealthy consumer was young—on average twenty years younger than their European, American, or Japanese counterparts with comparable purchasing power—and for the most part, much more educated than the rest of the Chinese population. Eager to consume, they were particularly open to foreign brands, symbols of social success. This was good news for the industry's major groups.

For François-Henri Pinault and Pinault-Printemps-Redoute's executive team, the future was in luxury, an activity with tremendous international growth potential. To reflect its global ambitions, the group decided to change its name. In May 2005, Pinault Printemps-Redoute became PPR, "a simpler, more international name," as the company emphasized in a press release. And it was with these two major retail brands, Printemps and La Redoute, that François-Henri Pinault decided to immediately begin refocusing on luxury, the second part of his strategy, and withdraw from consumer distribution, a business the group had entered with the acquisition of Conforama in 1991. Obviously well aware of these changes, François Pinault had complete confidence in his son's ability to negotiate this new strategic shift. "He gave me complete freedom to decide, telling me that it was up to me. Yet it was a question of continuing to undo what he had taken years to build. I admire his tremendous adaptability," says François-Henri Pinault.

The first divestment was completed in 2006. In August, the Printemps group, composed of eighteen stores including the flagship on Boulevard Haussmann, was sold to the Borletti family, owners of the Italian department stores Rinascente, and a subsidiary of Deutsche Bank. Analysts reacted favorably to the transaction, considering it as a sign of PPR's determination to refocus on luxury. The sale of Printemps was followed by that of the lingerie chain Orcanta, which was acquired by the Chantelle group.

Left: The former Pinault-Printemps-Redoute headquarters
on Place Henri Bergson, 8th arrondissement, Paris.
Right: The former PPR headquarters on Avenue Hoche,
8th arrondissement, Paris.

By the end of 2006, the "new PPR," to use the group's official expression, generated 80.1 percent of its revenue in retail and distribution, with CFAO, the Conforama and Fnac brands and the Redcats group, and nearly 20 percent in luxury. Going beyond strategic concerns, the retail and distribution division, particularly consumer brands, continued to experience significant growth. In 2006, Conforama took control of its main franchisee, Sodice Expansion, which operated fourteen stores, while Redcats acquired the American home-shopping company Sportsman's Guide, specializing in outdoor equipment and apparel. At the same time, Fnac accelerated its globalization by opening seven new stores outside France in 2007. The sales points of the Redcats group, like those of Fnac and Conforama, were also continually modernizing. All the brands were expanding their collections and improving the services they offered clients. Thus, the group continued to invest in retail and distribution. The idea was to withdraw eventually, but gradually.

In the process of refocusing on luxury, François-Henri Pinault was moving methodically, in stages, mindful to diversify both risks and sources of cash flow, which were essential for development. Indeed, the group had become accustomed to these long-term transformations, which are part of its identity. "The group's history is punctuated by changes spread over quite long periods," confirmed the leader of PPR in an interview with *Les Echos* in 2009.

A committed company

François-Henri Pinault's accelerated refocusing on luxury was not the only major change he set in motion. It was also at his initiative that the group launched an ambitious and committed policy of social and environmental responsibility (SER), founded on strong principles and with a long-term perspective. The actions implemented at that time concerned not only the group's governance but also led to significant philanthropic commitments. When François-Henri Pinault took the helm of Artémis in 2003, the group had already established benchmarks in this area. In 1990, for example, following the fire that ravaged Brocéliande Forest in Brittany, François Pinault had taken charge of its reforestation, under the direct supervision of the National Forestry Office. This was one of the first philanthropic actions undertaken by the Breton entrepreneur. Later, in 1996, Pinault-Printemps-Redoute established an Ethics Charter outlining the principles that should guide relations between the group's employees, as well as between the group and its external partners. Loyalty, integrity, transparency, fairness, respect, and trust are its watchwords. It is directly inspired by the management principles that François Pinault began following in 1962. In 2001, the group launched a new initiative, creating the association SolidarCité, with the aim of supporting the group's employees engaged in actions connected to social entrepreneurship and inclusivity.

In terms of SER, 2003 was clearly a watershed moment. At a time when Pinault-Printemps-Redoute was expressing its determination to conquer the world, especially through its Luxury division, the group adopted the standards used in major international groups, particularly in the United States. François-Henri Pinault's own convictions—being part of a generation that is more aware of these issues—were also instrumental and played

Jean-François Palus, Deputy CEO of PPR,
and François-Henri Pinault, President and CEO, in 2010.

a decisive role. From that point, initiatives within Pinault-Printemps-Redoute and then PPR multiplied and, in 2003, the group established a social and environmental responsibility office reporting to the human resources department. Its mission was to identify, through a network of correspondents in the field, the best practices in use within the group's various brands and companies, and to set shared objectives, particularly in terms of water and energy consumption, pollution reduction, and waste management. It was also the SER office that designed the group's new Code of Ethics, rolled out in 2005. Aligned with the 1996 Ethics Charter, it was designed to formalize PPR's commitments to its main stakeholders, both internal and external. Central to the Code is the fight against corruption and respect for human rights and diversity.

The group's approach to social responsibility has continued to evolve and become more coherent. In 2006, PPR structured its commitments around four unifying axes, which each brand used to create their own action plans: developing employees' skills, building lasting relationships with the group's partners and local communities, making the group's customers responsible actors, and reducing its environmental footprint. The following year, in 2007, the group took another major step by transforming the SER office into a full-fledged department, with its new manager, Laurent Claquin, joining the Executive Committee. This was a truly innovative move. "From that time, sustainability became a priority. To me, it seemed best that it be in the hands of a person directly connected to the president and a member of the Executive Committee. We became the first CAC 40 company to place sustainability at such a high level. No one really understood the point of this function. François-Henri Pinault immediately grasped its importance: he saw SER as a major strategic challenge and priority," says Laurent Claquin today.

Among the objectives of the new management team, there was one of prime importance: diversity. In 2004, PPR signed the Diversity Charter, published that year by the French think tank, Institut Montaigne, and along with some thirty major companies, the group worked to ensure the application of the principle of non-discrimination and to reflect French society's diversity. The same principles apply equally to people with disabilities. In 2004, PPR established a disabilities unit within the company. Its objective was to increase the number of employees with disabilities in its French operations from 3.2 to 6 percent by 2009. This goal was met and even exceeded by some brands, especially those in Redcats. But above anything else, PPR set an example with the representation of women within the group and its management bodies. In 2006, women represented 56 percent of the company's total workforce and more than 48 percent of managerial positions, compared with an average of 30 percent in other CAC 40 companies. In fact, before Printemps and Orcanta were sold, five women held positions as president or CEO. At the time, that was very unusual.

Supporting women was also the motivation for François-Henri Pinault's creation of the PPR Foundation for Women's Dignity and Rights, in January 2009. Partly inspired by actress, director and producer Salma Hayek, whom he married in 2009, it was completely in line with the structure of the group's workforce, as women comprised most of the group's employees and its clientele. The group's commitment to women made sense. The Foundation has two complementary objectives, realized notably through partnerships with nongovernmental organizations: on the one hand, to address violence against women—domestic violence, sexual violence and mutilation, trafficking, forced marriages, honor killings, etc.—and on the other, to support women's development projects, whether through vocational training, business creation, microcredit, or social entrepreneurship. At a time when the group was conducting an in-depth review of its business model, the Foundation strongly signaled the values on which it intended to pursue its expansion.

Top: François-Henri Pinault and Jochen Zeitz, CEO of Puma in
Germany, in 2007, at a press conference in Nuremberg announcing
PPR's acquisition of the German sporting brand.
Bottom: Jamaican athlete Usain Bolt, seconds after breaking the
100-meter world record at the 2008 Summer Olympics in Beijing.

LUXURY, SPORT & LIFESTYLE: PPR'S NEW FRONTIERS

In April 2007, PPR announced its takeover of the German sports equipment manufacturer Puma. This was the beginning of the creation of a new division within the group dedicated to Sport & Lifestyle, alongside Luxury.

Creating a Sport & Lifestyle division

Once again, the deal surprised observers who, thanks to persistent rumors, had expected the takeover of a luxury giant such as Hermès, Armani, or Bulgari. Yet the move was part of the group's carefully planned strategy, of which François-Henri Pinault now says: "Luxury didn't seem large enough to constitute our core activity, even if I was confident in its long-term growth potential. I considered developing our cosmetics business, which was already present in the group with Yves Saint Laurent Beauté. But this sector was already very concentrated and we were too small to make major acquisitions. On the other hand, we could imagine building another division alongside luxury, in the ready-to-wear and accessories sector. That's when the opportunity to buy Puma appeared. The Sport & Lifestyle sector corresponded to what we were looking for and had the advantage, like luxury, of being very international: the same products are sold all over the world." In fact, in sport as in luxury, the markets and stakes are global, with high-profile worldwide events and universal brands.

By taking control of Puma, PPR's intention was to become a leading group of global brands. François-Henri Pinault explained this very clearly in an interview given to *Les Echos* in November 2009. "Our strategic vision will enable us to build a group in the personal equipment sector, in the luxury and consumer segments, through strong brands and a growth model based, in part, on the control of our distribution networks," he said. Indeed, in the early 2010s, other acquisitions would be finalized.

The Puma takeover was to happen in two stages—a 27.1 percent stake first, quickly followed by a 62.1% stake—which corresponded with the objectives set by François-Henri Pinault. Created by Rudolf Dassler in 1948, Puma is a legendary brand. It is associated with the exploits of the greatest champions in the history of world sport, including Armin Hary, the fastest man in the world in 1960, Brazilian footballer Pelé, tennis players Guillermo Vilas and Boris Becker, and British sprinter Linford Christie, among many others. At the time of its acquisition by PPR, Puma partnered with Usain Bolt, who set world records in the 100 meters (9.69 seconds) and 200 meters (19.3 seconds) at the 2008 Olympic Games in Beijing. Puma was also a highly profitable company, with revenue of 2.4 billion euros in 2006. Its products, mostly sports shoes but also apparel and accessories, were distributed not only through multi-brand sports stores but also through its own retail network, with ninety stores worldwide, including forty in the United States. Finally, and this is a crucial point, the brand's target market was the general public and it had regularly collaborated with designers for its collections, including with those of the PPR group. In 2006, Puma launched a shoe collection by Alexander McQueen, the founder of the eponymous fashion House, which had become part of PPR's Luxury division. That collaboration received a lot of attention in the world of sport.

As soon as PPR acquired Puma, it began working to change the brand's positioning. The official mission was to make it "the most desirable and sustainable Sports & Lifestyle company in the world." Product ranges were expanded into new categories, a trend laboratory was created, and the partnership with Alexander McQueen was strengthened to offer collections at the intersection of fashion and sport. From 2007, Puma was moving upmarket, with the new goal of being highly sustainable. This was behind the PumaVision concept, developed in 2010, which established some bold objectives for the brand, such as a 25 percent reduction of polluting emissions and water and energy consumption by 2015. In 2010, Puma became the first company in the Sport & Lifestyle sector to join the United Nations Environment Programme's Climate Neutral Network, which aimed to reduce CO_2 emissions. The company also became the first in its industry to build a carbon-neutral building, the PumaVision headquarters in Herzogenaurach, Germany.

Becoming a world leader in luxury

Following the acquisition of Puma, PPR was organized into six operating divisions: Fnac, Redcats, Conforama, CFAO, the Gucci Group, and Puma. The first four still accounted for nearly 72 percent of revenue, compared to 19.6 percent for the Gucci Group and 8.6 percent for Puma. The Luxury and Sport & Lifestyle divisions, on the other hand, represented more than 55 percent of the group's operating income, including 41.7 percent for the Gucci Group alone, proving François-Henri Pinault's intuition: the future of PPR lay in global personal goods brands and, especially, luxury.

In parallel to forming a Sport & Lifestyle division, the group was also consolidating its Luxury division, which was now made up of leading brands—Gucci, Bottega Veneta, and Yves Saint Laurent—more specialized brands with strong growth potential—Balenciaga, Alexander McQueen, and Stella McCartney—and finally two recognized specialty brands—Boucheron (jewelry) and Sergio Rossi (footwear). Since Robert Polet's arrival in 2004, significant efforts had been made to give this portfolio new momentum. The group had begun pooling a number of noncreative functions and investing heavily in advertising and marketing. Various brands had also repositioned their collections to ensure their stature in the world of luxury and accentuate exclusiveness. For example, at Yves Saint Laurent, under the leadership of CEO Valérie Hermann and its Creative Director, Stefano Pilati, new leather goods lines were developed, including the *Muse*, *Downtown*, and *Besace* handbags and the successful *Tribute* line of shoes. At Balenciaga, CEO Isabelle Guichot and Artistic Director Nicolas Ghesquière concentrated on developing accessories and ready-to-wear, while Gucci intensified focus on its fundamental principles—creativity, quality, *made in Italy*, exclusivity—with the design of the fashion collections led by Frida Giannini, who was now the Italian House's sole creative director.

In keeping with its strategy to control distribution, one of its main objectives, the group concentrated on opening new, directly-owned stores. In 2007, it had 494, compared to 426 in 2005 and 398 in 2004. In 2008, there would be 560! Unsurprisingly, the group's priority was expansion into the emerging markets of South America, Russia, India, and especially China. At the end of 2007, Gucci—China's third-favorite brand according to a 2010 survey by Hong Kong newspaper *Wen Wei Po*—already operated twenty-five stores in Greater China. By the end of the following year, it would have thirty-three. The brand also opened a first store in India, in Mumbai. Bottega

Veneta initially moved into China in 2007, opening two stores, in Shanghai and Beijing. The United States was another important market. In February 2008, Gucci opened its new flagship in New York, a 4,000 square-meter store located at the corner of Fifth Avenue and 56th Street. A true "declaration of love to New York," as Gucci's CEO Mark Lee explained.

Strengthening PPR's Luxury division also involved acquisitions. This led to the group becoming interested in watchmaking. PPR had only Boucheron, and so was far behind Richemont and LVMH. In 2008, PPR acquired a 23 percent stake in the Sowind group, owner of the Swiss Luxury watch brand Girard-Perregaux.

At that time, however, the development of PPR's Luxury division was essentially based on the organic growth of its Houses. This strategy can also be linked to the sudden economic downturn in 2008.

A time of transformation

In particular, the crisis hit low-income American households that were unable to repay loans on their homes. Known as the subprime mortgage crisis due to the loans that were widely granted during the 2000s, it destabilized global finance before hitting the real economy. By the end of 2008, every sector was affected. Luxury was not immune: global sales fell 8 percent in 2009, the first drop since the early 1990s. The sector was much less affected by the crisis than other sectors of the economy, however. Its high margins and the vitality of the Chinese market, which grew 9.4 percent in 2009, enabled it to better withstand the downturn.

In the face of this precarious situation, however, PPR postponed investment projects and initiated cost reduction plans across its activities. Above all, it accelerated its focus on Luxury and Sport & Lifestyle. In April 2009, the group sold the computer equipment brand Surcouf, which had five stores in France, to Hugues Mulliez, founder of the IT products and services brand Youg's. A few months later, in November, it floated 58 percent of CFAO's capital on the stock market, thus initiating its exit from automobile and pharmaceutical distribution in Africa, which would become definitive in 2012. The IPO was the largest in Europe since 2007. In December 2010, the group announced that it was selling the furniture chain Conforama, with 241 stores in Europe, to the South African conglomerate Steinhoff. In parallel, PPR consolidated its Sport & Lifestyle division by acquiring the American golf equipment specialist Cobra in March 2010, through Puma. By then, the world's third-largest sportswear company, it had already been producing apparel and shoes for wearing on the green. Cobra's takeover allowed it to acquire technical legitimacy.

All these operations were profoundly changing PPR's profile. At the end of 2010, the Luxury and Sport & Lifestyle divisions accounted for 45 percent of revenue, including 27 percent for luxury goods, while the retail sector, now reduced to Fnac and Redcats, represented 55 percent. As well, the group's internationalization was accelerating with the growth of Luxury and Sport & Lifestyle. While in 2005, Western Europe, including France, accounted for 72 percent of PPR's revenue, in 2010 it represented only 59 percent, compared to 11 percent for Asia-Pacific, 6 percent for Japan, and 16 percent for North America. While there was still much to be done, there could be no doubt that the group was now fully, and successfully, global.

"We have charted a clear course, with specific objectives. We will continue to manage our business portfolios in line with our longer-term goals. This will involve strategic acquisitions in both the luxury goods and consumer markets. We will target iconic brands with international potential and values that have an authenticity more than being purely stylistic, such as Puma in the sports and lifestyle markets. We will continue to build a portfolio of brands offering high organic growth potential within the luxury/lifestyle segment, and existing in segments that do not compete with our own," said François-Henri Pinault in 2010 in an interview introducing the annual report for the 2009 fiscal year. The message was clear: PPR's transformation, which began in 2003, was about to enter its final phase.

2011: A pivotal year

For PPR, 2011 was a pivotal year. It was witness to major decisions that would have a lasting impact on the group's prospects. The first was the launch, in February, of a vast reorganization of the Luxury and the Sport & Lifestyle divisions, intended to form the basis of the future PPR.

This involved the merger of PPR and the Gucci Group, with the aim of blending the corporate teams of both entities into one simplified structure. The goal was to make PPR a truly integrated group by developing shared services and eliminating the repetition of support functions. It was at this time that Robert Polet left the Gucci Group, after seven years at the head of the Luxury division and a more than stellar record. He was succeeded by François-Henri Pinault. The CEO of PPR would now work directly with the heads of Gucci, Bottega Veneta, Yves Saint Laurent, and Balenciaga, while Alexis Babeau, named Deputy CEO of the Luxury division, would oversee the other brands. By taking over as head of luxury operations and removing the layer that had previously existed between him and the directors of the various brands, François-Henri Pinault's intention was to give the division new energy. It also underlined the highly strategic importance of luxury goods for the group.

This evolution involved an internal reorganization dubbed "One Team," founded on a simple principle: all functions related to products and customer relations would be autonomously managed by the brands; all back-office matters, including administrative, financial, legal, and IT matters, would be taken care of by the group as shared services.

Though the Gucci Group's integration into PPR reduced the autonomy of the luxury goods division, it did not fundamentally call into question the freedom various brands enjoyed under the leadership of their CEOs and creative directors. In fact, the division gained in efficiency and responsiveness. "One of François-Henri Pinault's objectives in merging the Gucci Group and PPR, and in taking over as head of the Luxury division, was to promote collaboration between the brands, to ensure the strategic coherence of their development, and to pool certain services in the pursuit of efficiency. Since that time, the Luxury division's major objectives have been defined at group level. They constitute the framework within which each brand has evolved," explains Marco Bizzarri, CEO of Gucci from 2015 to 2023. The group has dubbed this management style "Freedom within a framework."

Changes within the Luxury division were accompanied by the launch of a Sport & Lifestyle division, which had, in practice, existed since 2007, but was officially created in 2011. Led by Jochen Zeitz, the former CEO of Puma, it included the Puma and Cobra brands, with other PPR acquisitions to come. In May 2011, the group initiated a friendly takeover bid for the Nasdaq-listed American company Volcom. Founded in California in 1991 and specialized in apparel and accessories for board sports—skateboarding, surfing, and snowboarding—the company also produced sports glasses through its subsidiary Electric Visual. With 70 percent of its revenue generated in the United States, Volcom was clearly not on the same scale as a global brand like Quiksilver. Nevertheless, it had strong growth potential, particularly in Asia. This was one of the reasons PPR wanted to take control. In the Sport & Lifestyle arena, the group intended to be a "developer," focusing on brands with a solid capacity for international growth.

Exiting distribution

The group's extensive reorganization in 2011 had a very clear objective: to finalize PPR's exit from distribution and complete its refocus on Luxury and Sport & Lifestyle. In reality, the process really accelerated from 2012. That year, in addition to the sale of its remaining stake in CFAO, in quick succession the group announced its demerger from Fnac and its next IPO—which would be completed in June 2013—as well as the sale of Redcats' activities in the United States, which included Sportsman's Guide, The Golf Warehouse, and the plus-size specialist OneStopPlus. The process continued in 2013, with the sale of Redcats' children's and family divisions (Cyrillus and Vertbaudet) along with its Scandinavian business activities.

The final act came in 2014. In June of that year, Kering—the group's name since 2013, a subject we will return to—announced the sale of La Redoute and Relais Colis to their directors, Nathalie Balla and Éric Courteille. For a symbolic euro they acquired the two companies, whose revenue was 3 billion euros. But the group had put almost half a billion euros on the table: this sum would make it possible for the new owners to finance a major restructuring, which included a social component, including redundancies for the 1,178 jobs to be eliminated, especially in the group's mail-order warehouses, but also the construction of an ultramodern logistics center in Wattrelos, which would let the companies compete with the giants of e-commerce. In this case, Kering was acting responsibly, with the desire to ensure the mail-order company's survival and allow it to begin anew on solid foundations. In the years that followed, the success of its relaunch proved the company right.

In mid-2014, Kering definitively completed its transformation into an apparel and accessories specialist. A new chapter, following that of professional distribution, had begun in the history of the group. "Previously, we were a financial and operational conglomerate. Now we are an integrated and industrial entity dedicated to a single sector, apparel and accessories, via two threads, Luxury and Sport & Lifestyle," said François-Henri Pinault at a press conference in October 2012, when the withdrawal from consumer retail was well underway. Two years later, 66 percent of the group's revenue, which exceeded 10 billion euros, was generated through luxury and 34 percent via Sport & Lifestyle. Even as the latter was strengthened in the early 2010s with the acquisitions of Cobra, Volcom, and Electric Visual, the former experienced a phenomenal surge.

Luxury: The rise to power

The Gucci Group's integration into PPR launched a new era for the group's Luxury division. In 2011, François-Henri Pinault defined the strategic roadmap: developments in Luxury and in Sport & Lifestyle would be as much through internal (or "organic") growth as external development. With the sale of its consumer retail activities, the group had the resources to achieve its ambitions. Of course, the goal was to take full advantage of the booming luxury market. Since the beginning of the decade, its growth had outpaced that of the global economy—averaging 6 percent annually. Between 2010 and 2018, the years when the group would become a pure player in the luxury market, its revenue rose from 167 to 262 billion euros. The market shift to Asia, which had begun several years earlier, continued to gain momentum. The burgeoning importance of this part of the world, and especially China, to the growth of the luxury industry, can be summarized in a few figures: in 2010, Chinese customers accounted for about 15 percent of luxury purchases worldwide, behind European, American, and Japanese customers. In 2018, its share had risen to 33 percent, leading American (22 percent), European (18 percent), and Japanese (10 percent) customers. While China was not yet the world's top luxury market in terms of sales volume—Europe and the United States continued to lead the race—it was well on its way to surpassing them.

Everything was coming together to establish Chinese consumers as the sector's driving force. First, there was the gradual arrival of millennials, the generation born in the 1980s and 1990s. According to some studies, by the end of the 2010s they already represented 70 percent of Chinese luxury goods buyers. With their high spending power, they were particularly fond of brands and open to new trends, in particular the convergence of sport and fashion. But there was another phenomenon helping to drive sales in the sector: the increase in Chinese tourism. Between 2014 and 2018, the number of Chinese nationals traveling the globe increased from 60 to 150 million. They, too, are big buyers of luxury goods. A Bain & Company study estimated their spending in this sector alone at 75 billion euros in 2015, versus 6.5 billion ten years earlier.

There were challenges facing the strategy François-Henri Pinault defined in 2011: capitalizing on the market's global expansion, but also on the growing appetite of Chinese consumers for luxury products. Regarding external growth, priority was given to small and medium-sized brands, which, while not necessarily playing an immediate role in the value creation strategy, were nevertheless a catalyst for evolution and globalization. The aim was to buy brands with strong identities, values, and unique core expressions, as well as the ability to gradually expand beyond their home market. An original strategy compared to other luxury players, who had been more interested in major brands. "Buying a very large and very expensive brand does not create value for the shareholder," noted François-Henri Pinault in an interview with *Les Echos* in November 2011.

These principles were reflected in the acquisition of Italy's Brioni, announced in 2011 and finalized in 2012. Founded in 1945 by tailor Nazareno Fonticoli and entrepreneur Gaetano Savini, the high-end men's clothing specialist was certainly modest but its suits were renowned, sought after by Hollywood A-listers and world leaders alike. With seventy-four stores, Brioni already had a strong international base: 39 percent of its revenue was generated in Europe, 29 percent in North America, and 23 percent in Asia.

It therefore had significant potential for growth. With its acquisition, PPR decided to accelerate its expansion in Asia.

A year later, in 2012, PPR announced a new acquisition, that of the young Chinese jewelry brand Qeelin. The deal, which again represented a daring move, allowed the group to consolidate its foothold in jewelry, a sector in which Boucheron was its only representative. On the one hand, this was the group's first acquisition in China; on the other hand, Qeelin was relatively small, with only fourteen stores—eleven in China, one in Paris, and two in London—and revenue of around 30 million euros. But the brand also had a lot to offer. Founded by Chinese designer Dennis Chan, its creations had a clear identity: they were contemporary reinterpretations of symbols inherited from time-honored Chinese legends. Above all, its acquisition allowed the group to strengthen its position in the Chinese market. PPR also announced its intention to accelerate store openings in Mainland China and in Hong Kong.

Acquisitions gathered momentum in 2013. That year, the group, which had just taken the name Kering, announced the purchase of the Italian jeweler Pomellato. Founded in Milan in 1967, Pomellato was one of the last independent jewelry groups in Europe. Its founder, Pino Rabolini, was the first to introduce the idea of ready-to-wear into the world of jewelry, giving the brand a strong, distinctive identity. Best known for its rings with colored stones, Pomellato also operated the brand DoDo. Through its eighty-five stores, fifty-five of which were directly operated, the company could be found in major European capitals, the United States, Asia, and the Middle East. Its potential for development was immense.

That same year, Kering acquired a 51 percent stake in the luxury ready-to-wear brand Christopher Kane, founded in 2004 by the Scottish designer of the same name. Though the brand did not yet have its own store, it was distributed in thirty countries through a network of 150 sales points operated by third parties. In 2013, the British Fashion Council (BFC) named Christopher Kane Womenswear Designer of the Year at the British Fashion Awards, further enhancing his profile.

In 2014, a final acquisition of the Ulysse Nardin brand expanded the group's Luxury division, this time in the field of fine watchmaking. Founded in 1846 and anchored in the marine world, the Swiss manufacturer utilizes innovative technical expertise to create chronometers and grand complications. Distributed through twenty directly-owned stores and a network of specialized watch boutiques, Ulysse Nardin was most visible in North America and Russia. Like the other brands acquired by the group, it had significant growth potential, especially in Asia.

In the space of five years, the group had strengthened its multi-brand model by enriching its Luxury division with new houses, each with a specific identity and strong development potential. Its portfolio now counted fourteen Houses, which formed a coherent and complementary whole, particularly in terms of market segments. A resolutely pursued strategy of targeted acquisitions was accompanied by vigorous organic growth, with the opening of new directly-owned stores in major international capitals and emerging markets—no fewer than 377 between 2012 and 2017, across all the brands—and the upmarket shift in the range of products offered, as well as the entry into new universes, for example with Bottega Veneta. The group acted on every front, in order to, in its own words, "harness the full potential of luxury and grow faster than the market." These developments allowed the group to affirm its vision of "embracing creativity for a modern, bold vision of luxury." Through its different brands, the group's intention was to set trends: to achieve this, it dared to "take risks, think differently, and constantly propose fresh and innovative ideas." And indeed, it was taking risks, especially in the choice of its artistic directors.

The years 2010 to 2015 were defined by the arrival of a new generation of designers. All were chosen or endorsed by François-Henri Pinault himself, who never hesitated to bet on atypical personalities. In 2010, after the tragic death of Alexander McQueen, he entrusted the artistic direction of the House to Sarah Burton, Head of Womenswear. In 2011, she designed the bridal gown Kate Middleton wore for her wedding to Prince William at Westminster Abbey. More generally, that same year, the originality of her creations earned her the British Fashion Council's award for British Designer of the Year; in 2012, she was named Best International Designer by the Elle Style Awards.

There was also a revival afoot at Yves Saint Laurent, when in 2012 François-Henri Pinault entrusted the artistic direction to Hedi Slimane, the former Creative Director at Dior Homme, replacing Stefano Pilati. He launched a major shift, renaming the brand "Saint Laurent" and introducing a new rock aesthetic that contributed to the prestigious label's rebirth. Even more unexpected was Demna Gvasalia's arrival at Balenciaga in 2015, replacing Alexander Wang. Little known to the general public despite launching his own buzzy fashion label Vetements, this Georgian-born stylist overturned the brand's codes. In early 2015, Marco Bizzarri chose Alessandro Michele to succeed Frida Giannini as Creative Director of Gucci. Like Sarah Burton at Alexander McQueen, he came from in-house. Having joined Gucci in 2002, he had held several positions, including creative director of leather goods. It took him less than a year to transform the House, moving it once again into fashion's epicenter. Lastly, in 2016 Anthony Vaccarello succeeded Hedi Slimane at Saint Laurent, expanding the Parisian House's revival. With the arrival of these new designers at Gucci, Saint Laurent, Balenciaga, and Alexander McQueen, Kering resolutely asserted its singularity and its difference in the luxury world.

A more integrated Luxury division

In 2017, Kering's Luxury division looked very different than it had just five or six years before. From a financial perspective, it was worth just over 10 billion euros, or nearly 70 percent of the entire group's revenue (15.2 billion euros). Sales in Western Europe represented 33 percent, Asia-Pacific 27 percent, North America 21 percent, Japan 8 percent, and the rest of the world 11 percent. The division counted 1,388 directly-owned stores, including 367 in Western Europe, 219 in the United States, 260 in Japan, and 542 in emerging countries. More than ever, China represented a potential market for the group, which continued its heavy investments there. It also made highly symbolic gestures. This included the 2013 decision by François Pinault and François-Henri Pinault to return to China two bronze animal heads dating from the reign of the Qianlong Emperor (1736–95), which had been taken from the Zodiac fountain in the Summer Palace in Beijing when it was ransacked by British and French troops during the Second Opium War in 1860. Previously part of the Yves Saint Laurent and Pierre Bergé collections, they were auctioned in 2009 by Christie's, which Artémis has owned since 1998,

Nazareno Fonticoli and Gaetano Savini,
founders of the House of Brioni.

Left: The first Qeelin store in Paris, at Palais Royal, 1999.
Right: Dennis Chan, founder of Qeelin.

and bought by the Pinault family to donate to their country of origin. This gesture sent a strong message to China. Announced by François-Henri Pinault in April 2013, at a state dinner given during President François Hollande's visit to China, the restitution of the two artworks was effected during a special ceremony a few weeks later.

"In 2015, the group entered a new phase of structural reorganization. The challenge was to improve what was already in place, to professionalize the teams, and to clearly define the balance between the autonomy of the brands and the group's involvement," says Jean-Marc Duplaix, the group's Financial Director since 2012. In 2015, the luxury business was structured around three divisions: Couture & Leather Goods, including the Gucci, Bottega Veneta, and Saint Laurent brands; emerging brands, with Balenciaga, Alexander McQueen, Stella McCartney, Christopher Kane, and Brioni; and finally, Watches & Jewelry, with Boucheron, Pomellato (which also manages the brand DoDo), Qeelin, Girard-Perregaux, and Ulysse Nardin. This organization was intended to reflect the specificity of each House and better respond to their needs according to their stage of development. It was also characterized by more operational expertise. This integrative approach can also be seen in the 2013 acquisition of France Croco, one of France's leading independent tanneries, specializing in the treatment and processing of exotic skins. It would supply all the group's brands with high-quality exotic leathers.

More surprising—and innovative—was the creation of Kering Eyewear in 2014. This new company was in keeping with the integration strategy that Kering intended to follow. Its purpose was to bring together all the group's eyewear expertise, whereas traditionally the Houses themselves had managed that sector through licenses with specialized outside partners. The idea of an internal entity dedicated to eyewear was relatively new in the luxury industry. With Kering Eyewear, the group intended to develop its own expertise by internalizing the eyewear business's value chain, from design to production, distribution, and marketing. Created and led by Roberto Vedovotto, this new entity brought together collections designed by Bottega Veneta, Saint Laurent, Alexander McQueen, Stella McCartney, Boucheron, and Puma. It began as a genuine start-up. "We launched with four people. We had no office, no Wi-Fi, no cell phones, and no revenue. Everything had to be built. We started from scratch, relying on our main assets—our brand portfolio and our audacity—to transform the industry's traditional business model," recounts Roberto Vedovotto. Kering Eyewear was an immediate success: by 2022, its revenue exceeded 1.1 billion euros and it employed just over 3,800 people. "In my opinion, Kering Eyewear symbolizes the entrepreneurial spirit that is always at play within the group," concludes Roberto Vedovotto.

And then, of course, there was digital. In this domain, the group had clearly been a pioneer, launching e-commerce sites within its retail distribution businesses in the mid-1990s, among the first in France. Gucci had also been an early innovator, creating one of the luxury industry's very first e-commerce sites in 2002. Ten years later, digital had become a major challenge for luxury. In fact, since 2010, online sales had been growing faster than in-store sales—27 percent on average compared to 7 percent. Between 2014 and 2018, global online sales of luxury goods increased from 5 percent to more than 10 percent of the market. Once again, the dynamism of the Chinese market set it apart. Since the early 2010s, largely thanks to millennials, an overwhelmingly digital generation, online sales experienced double-digit growth rates, in this case +71 percent between 2011 and 2012 according to the newspaper *Les Echos*, citing a Boston Consulting Group study published in late 2012. Faced with digital's rising power, the PPR group once again had a big task ahead. In 2011, e-commerce represented less than 4 percent of its global luxury sales, with Gucci accounting for the largest share. Recognizing that its other brands did not have access to the same resources as its flagship company to develop their own online offering, the group decided to create a shared e-business platform, providing the technical capabilities to deploy individual digital strategies. That was the purpose of the joint venture created in August 2012 with Italian company Yoox, a leader in luxury e-commerce. Present in approximately one hundred countries, including China of course, Yoox already operated the online presence of some thirty labels. With 51 percent controlled by PPR, the joint venture would manage online stores for the group's brands, which would retain exclusive control of products and image. The goal was to increase the share of online sales to 10 percent by 2015. Kering would then be able to recover, in a second phase, direct control of this strategic activity.

Between 2011 and 2017, Kering's Luxury division experienced rapid growth. In 2017, luxury accounted for 70 percent of Kering's revenue and more than 90 percent of its operating income. These numbers meant that the group had nearly completed its conversion into a pure player in the luxury industry. François-Henri Pinault had been preparing for this for some time. It would take another two years to accomplish this new strategic transformation.

François Pinault and François-Henri Pinault in 2013 during
the celebration commemorating the return to China of two sculptures
from the Zodiac fountain in the former Summer Palace in Beijing.

Presentation of Kering Eyewear's "Collezione Uno" in Venice in 2015,
during the official launch of the entity Kering created the previous year.

A Global Luxury Giant

Kering's Material Innovation Lab in Milan, Italy.

A new name, a new location, a new image, a renewed commitment to its ambitions in terms of sustainability and social responsibility. From 2013, while accelerating the development of its Luxury division, the group thoroughly restructured its identity, which was now more in line with its profile and mission.

A new name, an iconic new home

On June 18, 2013, at the Annual General Meeting to approve the previous year's financial statements, PPR officially took the name Kering. François-Henri Pinault had been thinking about this change since 2011, when PPR merged with the Gucci Group. The sale of Printemps in 2006, and the future sale of La Redoute—the deal would be finalized in 2014—required a new name for the group that was better suited to its activities in Luxury and Sport & Lifestyle, but also to its international scope. The objective was to break with the image of a financial conglomerate that the name PPR still conveyed. François-Henri Pinault summed up these challenges in an interview with the *Journal du Dimanche* in March 2013: "In fifty years, we have gone from a conglomerate to a global group focused on apparel and accessories. France represents only 5 percent of revenue. Emerging countries, particularly China, are driving the market, and sales in the United States remain dynamic. In 1988, only one American worked at our headquarters. Today, there are seventeen nationalities working together." As to the disappearance of the Pinault name, that was perhaps surprising given that its family dimension—the group has been owned and run by the family since its creation in 1962—is part of its DNA. However, its loss was a response to a very specific objective. "I decided to not keep the Pinault name because if one day I make mistakes, my loved ones would not suffer the consequences. Conversely, a family may experience problems that can negatively impact the business. My father agrees with this decision," explains François-Henri Pinault.

Introduced in March 2013, the Kering name reflects these transformations and the requirements now underpinning the group's development. It is a name rich in meaning. "Kering can be pronounced and understood as 'caring.' Kering stands for more than a change in scope or activity. The new name describes our distinctive attitude toward our brands, people, customers, stakeholders, and the environment. The change of name is also an opportunity to reaffirm the group's international dimension while acknowledging its origins in the Brittany region of France. In the Breton language *ker* means 'home.' Kering is therefore the family home that our brands and our employees inhabit."

"Our new emblem is an owl, the sign of wisdom. It represents the visionary side of the group, our ability to anticipate trends and spot potential. A discreet and protective animal, it is a powerful symbol for a company that guides and nurtures its brands and people," the group explained when it presented its new identity to shareholders. The group also adopted a Chinese name: "kai yun," whose associated ideograms mean "sky that clears and opens all possibilities." These words bode well for a group that has made the Chinese market one of its priorities.

The launch of the new identity was accompanied by a new tagline: "Empowering Imagination." Introduced in 2013, it illustrates how the group intends to create value by encouraging imagination in all its forms, to spark initiatives, stimulate the creativity of its Houses and support their growth. "Empowering Imagination means putting creation at the heart of everything we do. By entrusting our Houses to uniquely talented individuals and giving them total creative freedom, a guarantee of creative risk-taking and sincerity. Empowering Imagination means enabling our Houses to continually push beyond their limits. By building an agile and integrated group that creates significant value. Empowering Imagination is about cultivating talent and promoting a culture of entrepreneurship. It also means committing our imagination to sustainable and responsible luxury," Kering explained in its 2017 activity report. The signature carries both a promise and an expression of a vision, that of modern, moving, creative, and daring luxury that inspires the entire industry.

The new identity reflects the company's transformation, which had been underway for several years, into an integrated, coherent, and international group. Moving the head office to the former Laennec Hospital, located at 40 Rue de Sèvres in the 7th arrondissement of Paris, was part of this transformation. At the beginning of the 2010s, the group's headquarters had been established on Avenue Hoche. Although not lacking in prestige, the spaces occupied were purely functional. In search of a unique site to gather his teams and House Balenciaga, which did not have enough space, François-Henri Pinault visited the Laennec site. Built in the seventeenth century and a classified historical monument, the former hospital was undergoing major reconstruction, overseen by France's Monuments Historiques, in order to build housing and offices. "It was a total aesthetic shock. Although we weren't looking for a large site, at the end of the visit, I said that we'd take everything," François-Henri Pinault told the newspaper *Le Figaro* in September 2016.

Scheduled for 2014, the move ultimately took place in 2016 due to prolonged renovations. Between them, the headquarters of Kering and Balenciaga occupy 18,2986 square feet (17,000 square meters). There is an additional benefit: the old hospital is one of the few historical monuments in France to receive the stringent HQE (High Environmental Quality) certification.

The new site completely reflects the group's image. "In our luxury businesses, historical roots are essential. Taking up residence here reasserts our Parisian and French roots. We took the name Kering and "ker" means 'home' and 'place of life' in Breton. And now we also own a house. In its singularity and audacity, this place resembles us. It is the place for a different luxury that is free to make its own choices," François-Henri Pinault emphasized in the interview with *Le Figaro*. More broadly, the group's arrival on Rue de Sèvres opened a new era in the way it manages its image. That same year, in 2016, Valérie Duport joined Kering as Chief Communications and Image Officer after twenty-seven years at Chanel. "When I arrived, the group was completely evolving," she remembers today. "There was a gap between its new profile and its identity, which was still characterized by the financial image associated with PPR. Kering had to move from a collection of luxury brands to a luxury group. This meant that from then on, image and communication were key."

Poster for the film *Home* by Yann Arthus-Bertrand, a documentary supported by PPR; since 2009, it has been watched by some 800 million people.

PPR présente
NOUS AVONS TOUS RENDEZ-VOUS
AVEC LA PLANETE LE 5 JUIN !
HOME
UN FILM DE
YANN ARTHUS-BERTRAND
AVEC LA VOIX DE JACQUES GAMBLIN SCÉNARIO ISABELLE DELANNOY YANN ARTHUS-BERTRAND YEN LE VAN COMMENTAIRE ISABELLE DELANNOY
ARTHUS-BERTRAND CHEF MONTEUSE YEN LE VAN ASSISTANTE RÉALISATEUR DOROTHÉE MARTIN CAMERAMAN DIRECTEUR DE PRODUCTION JEAN DE TREGOMAIN
COORDINATRICE CAMILLE COURAU PRODUIT PAR DENIS CAROT ET LUC BESSON
© 2009 - EUROPACORP - ELZEVIR FILMS
PPR
UNEP
www.home-2009.com
EUROPACORP

A leader in sustainable development

"To be a responsible group." Kering had been making that promise for a long time, since it presented its first Ethics Charter in 1996. Then, as mentioned, came the creation of a sustainability unit at the group level in 2003, which became a full-fledged department reporting to its president in 2007. In 2009, there followed the creation of the PPR Foundation for Women's Dignity and Rights, which in 2013 became the Kering Foundation. In 2009, the group also financed Yann Arthus-Bertrand's film *Home*, which tracked the state of the Earth from the sky, demonstrating the group's commitment to protecting the environment.

In the early 2010s, with the refocusing on personal goods and the very rapid growth in luxury goods, the group strongly reasserted its ambitions: Kering's intention was to promote "responsible and sustainable luxury." Far from being considered a constraint, sustainability was seen as a competitive advantage to ensure the group's future. Numerous initiatives were launched during that decade, which saw many important changes for the enterprise. Among the most important: in 2012, the group defined a series of structural and ambitious sustainability objectives to be achieved by 2016. Involving all brands in a process of continuous progress, these objectives focused on key areas in terms of environmental footprint, the sourcing of raw materials, and ethical compliance. Three years later, an Environmental Profit & Loss (EP&L) statement, first published by Puma in 2011, was rolled out across the entire group. This pioneering tool measures the impact of the group's activities on the planet, examining the entire value chain, particularly upstream of Kering's statutory limits along its supply chain. Its deployment was accompanied by concrete measures, including the search for new supply sources along with the development of innovative processes and products with improved social and environmental balance. For example, since 2013 Gucci and Bottega Veneta have been working on tanning leather using methods that are free of heavy metals, reducing leather production's impact on nature. That same year saw the creation of the Material Innovation Lab (MIL), a library of sustainable fabrics and textiles available to the creative teams of the group's Houses. In 2017, Kering took an important step, publishing its 2025 Sustainability Strategy. The objectives were ambitious: they demanded a significant 40 percent reduction in the group's environmental impact, from the supply of raw materials to transport and manufacturing. Kering's roadmap extended beyond the environmental dimension, integrating a major social component and strengthening the role of innovation in its sustainable development strategy. The progress report in 2020 was more than encouraging. At that point, greenhouse gas emissions linked to stores had reduced by 77 percent, while the gold used in Kering's watches and jewelry was now all responsibly sourced. Three years later, the group was able to announce even more significant progress: Kering had reduced its overall environmental impact by 40 percent, reaching its target four years ahead of schedule. Between 2015 and 2022, the group reduced its overall emissions of scopes 1 and 2 of the Greenhouse Gas Protocol, and lowered the intensity of its Scope 3 emissions by 52 percent. It now uses 100 percent renewable electricity and has attained 95 percent traceability for its main raw materials.

Not content with these numbers, Kering's sustainable development team has become involved in new areas, including regenerative agriculture and sustainable finance. In 2021, Kering announced another landmark measure: it became the first luxury group to completely stop using fur. And in

François-Henri Pinault and French President
Emmanuel Macron in 2019, during the launch
of The Fashion Pact at the Élysée Palace.

In 2019, Kering paid tribute to Agnès Varda
on the official Women In Motion poster for
the 72nd edition of the Festival de Cannes.
That same year, Kering and the Rencontres
d'Arles awarded the first Women In Motion Award for
photography to American photographer Susan Meiselas.

March 2023, Kering set a very new, very ambitious goal: to move from reducing the carbon intensity of its operations to reducing emissions in absolute terms, and to cut them by 40 percent by 2035. "I am convinced that the next stage in building truly sustainable companies is reducing our impact in absolute terms while creating value," says François-Henri Pinault.

To create value, Kering is also working to attract the best people. "Developing talent is at the heart of our strategy and our culture," says Béatrice Lazat, the group's Chief People Officer. "We provide our teams with inspiration, with the resources and work environment to enable them to be bold, ambitious, and tenacious. In real terms, it is just as much about ensuring the well-being of our employees as it is about giving them the latitude to exercise an entrepreneurial spirit, and encouraging creativity and risk-taking."

Kering has also been determined to assiduously reaffirm its mission in terms of inclusivity and social good. In 2005, François-Henri Pinault's arrival at the head of the group meant an acceleration in that respect. In 2016, following the various initiatives carried out over the previous decade, Kering was awarded the GEEIS (Gender Equality European & International Standard) label by the Arborus Endowment Fund, the world's first fund to support professional equality, a recognition of the group's commitment to equality in the workplace. Three years later, in 2019, the group was ranked tenth among 7,000 international companies in the global Thomson Reuters Diversity & Inclusion Index. In terms of parity, Kering ranks among industry leaders. In 2022, women represented 63 percent of the group's total workforce, accounting for 57 percent of its management, 33 percent of its Executive Committee, and 45 percent of its Board of Directors. These results are far above the French national average for companies of comparable size, which report only 33.7 percent for management and 20.3 percent for executive committees.

Supporting the advancement of women is one of the group's priorities. The Kering Foundation is, of course, evidence of this, as is the 2017 launch of a working relations charter for the well-being of models, both female and male, in collaboration with LVMH. The commitments made by the two groups, in particular the ban on models who are too thin, go well beyond France's legal provisions concerning the profession. The goal is to establish shared standards for all players in the fashion industry.

Another pillar of the group's commitment to women is the program Women In Motion. Launched in 2015 in partnership with the Festival de Cannes, its mission is to highlight the role and contribution of women in cinema. An award for photography was added in 2016, the year in which Kering partnered with the Rencontres d'Arles photography festival and the Kyotographie festival in Japan. Moreover, Women In Motion has contributed to changing ideas and has become a force for elevating women's place in the arts and culture on a global scale. Through its awards, the program also recognizes emerging female talent and inspiring figures, such as the actors and producers Susan Sarandon and Geena Davis in 2016, director Patty Jenkins in 2018, photographer Susan Meiselas in 2019, and Sabine Weiss in 2020.

Convinced that "sustainable business is smart business," Kering has placed sustainability and social and environmental responsibility among the major cornerstones of its policy. All the major players in the sector now share this commitment. "Luxury must be best-in-class," says Erwan Rambourg, a specialist in the sector and the author of the book *Future Luxe*, published in 2020. Because it reflects society's values and expectations, the luxury industry must demonstrate increasing responsibility in the face of environmental and social challenges. In addition, customers demand it, especially the youngest, who are looking for meaning and who expect companies to make genuine commitments in that area. While Kering is part of a broader movement, it also stands apart thanks to its pioneering commitments. By setting very ambitious goals and regularly sharing its progress, the group's intention is to change the way it designs products and to thoroughly rethink its relationships with customers, partners, and suppliers.

The group's commitments have been recognized and welcomed by NGOs and rating agencies. In 2022, the Canadian magazine *Corporate Knights* ranked Kering among the one hundred most exemplary groups in terms of sustainable development, and first in the Textiles, Apparel & Luxury Goods sector. For the tenth consecutive year, it also ranked among the industry leaders in the Dow Jones Sustainability Index (DJSI), World & Europe, in the textile, apparel, and luxury goods sector.

"The very positive way Kering is perceived by the media and by environmental associations, but also by financial analysts on environmental issues, is significant, encouraging, and unusual. Structurally, this isn't our industry's core business, but François-Henri Pinault has chosen this benchmark and is determined to ensure that Kering is *the* leading group in sustainable development within our industry, and that it is identified as a pioneer across sectors. Sustainability is treated with the utmost seriousness because it is at the heart of the group's strategy. This is in keeping with its uncompromising ethics and strong values. These very deep convictions are conceptualized, structured, and implemented in a personalized and operational approach within each of the group's companies," explains Marie-Claire Daveu, the group's Chief Sustainability Officer and Head of International Institutional Affairs since 2012.

As part of its commitment to sustainable development,
the Kering group supports programs connected to
biodiversity, including in French Guiana and Mongolia.

The Bottega Veneta store in Tokyo's Ginza district.

A PURE PLAYER
IN LUXURY

In January 2018, Kering announced that it was selling 70 percent of Puma's capital. With this operation, followed by the sale of Volcom a year later, the group divested its Sport & Lifestyle division, completing its transformation into a pure luxury player.

Selling the Sport & Lifestyle division: A culmination

The announcement of the sale of Puma, which foreshadowed that of the entire Sport & Lifestyle division, was not really a surprise. It was expected and hoped for by financial analysts; François-Henri Pinault himself had been preparing for this shift for some time. With the tremendous expansion of Kering's Luxury division, on which the majority of the group's profits were based, this activity no longer held its initial strategic character. While Puma had made a strong recovery since its acquisition in 2007, its performance, like that of Volcom, was not comparable to the luxury brands. Operating in a highly competitive sector, the brands in the Sport & Lifestyle division were also a very different model compared to those in luxury. It operates in the mass market, where major sporting goods retailers have a strong negotiating position. "Puma was no longer consistent with Kering's luxury activities. The brand, moreover, had gone through a complex phase of recovery. The group's leaders concluded that the time had come to focus exclusively on luxury, which was experiencing phenomenal growth," says Jean-Marc Duplaix.

A new stage in Kering's history, the sale of Puma took the form of a demerger and a redistribution of shares to shareholders, as had been the case with Fnac. Artémis would remain a major shareholder in the sports brand. This deal, which was followed by the sale of Volcom to Authentic Brands Group in 2019, marked the culmination of a concentration on luxury that began in 2011, and which has continued growing over the years. In the year Puma was sold, 2018, Kering's transformation was complete; it had become a pure player in luxury. With revenue of 13.7 billion euros, of which 20 percent was in North America, 33 percent in Western Europe, and 40 percent in Asia-Pacific, including Japan, and with 30,500 employees, it was organized around a portfolio of prestigious brands. In terms of market sectors, leather goods were well ahead (53 percent), followed by footwear (18 percent), ready-to-wear (15 percent), jewelry and watches (7%), and other categories (7%). By refocusing on luxury, Kering was also completing its transformation into an integrated group, a shift that had been underway for some time.

"By becoming a pure player specialized in a single business, we have ceased to be a holding company to become an integrated group. Decentralization, trust, and delegation remain, in relation to the brands. They make their own decisions about their products, for example. The five major brands report directly to me, the others to Jean-François Palus. But we have also set up, under the leadership of Jean-François, shared services, pooled centers of expertise, and growth platforms, meaning companies are able to focus on their core business while improving their efficiency and impact. Kering also helps them nurture a pool of talent attracted by the careers that an integrated group can offer. Thus, for example, since 2015 or 2016 almost all of our brand presidents have been appointed internally," explains François-Henri Pinault.

Luxury in motion

As one of the world's luxury leaders, Kering is committed to actively developing in every market where it operates. "Favoring organic growth, to take advantage of opportunities created by the expansion of luxury to a global scale," is the strategy François-Henri Pinault defined following the sale of the Sport & Lifestyle division. The first step was achieved mainly because of the relevancy of the brand portfolio. The decision was made to focus on the largest and most profitable Houses, meaning divesting smaller brands for which the group's structure was often too large. Thus, in 2018, Kering announced the end of its collaboration with Stella McCartney, who then took back the 50 percent stake that the group had held in the company she founded in 2001. A House that Kering had been instrumental in helping to grow, and now found in seventy-seven countries with fifty-two stores and more than 860 retail outlets. That same year, the group sold back to Christopher Kane the 51 percent stake it had held in his namesake brand since 2013. It also ended the partnership, established that same year, with Tomas Maier, then Artistic Director of Bottega Veneta, to create his own label.

Following these initiatives, the group's portfolio comprised eleven brands, excluding Kering Eyewear: Gucci, Saint Laurent, Bottega Veneta, Balenciaga, Alexander McQueen, Brioni, Boucheron, Pomellato, Qeelin, Ulysse Nardin, and Girard-Perregaux. Since their acquisition by Kering, most of these brands have grown quickly under the initiatives of their artistic directors and a new generation of leaders; they have also completely changed scale by setting out to conquer the world's major markets, especially Asia, expanding their network of directly-owned stores and evolving their collections. This was especially the case for Gucci. The 2004 departure of Domenico De Sole and Tom Ford changed the destiny of this prestigious Italian House. From the mid-2000s, its evolution picked up speed; in the space of ten years, from 2004 to 2014, the number of directly-owned stores rose from 198 to 505. The arrival of Marco Bizzarri at the company's helm in 2015 brought a new spirit. Guided by his leadership, and under the creative direction of Alessandro Michele, Gucci rode an extraordinary creative and commercial wave, signaling one of luxury's all-time greatest international success stories. "Gucci needed to reassert its fashion authority and return to the spotlight of fashion," explains Marco Bizzarri. "In only a few years, Gucci repurposed luxury by celebrating creativity, its Italian craftsmanship and innovation, as well as expanding its audience to new generations." From both a creative and commercial standpoint, extraordinary results would ensue for Italy's household name, heralding one of the most remarkable success stories in luxury the world over. In the period spanning 2015 and 2021, Gucci's revenue tripled from €3,8 to €10,5 billion.

The evolution at Saint Laurent was similar. Long gone were the days when the House counted only sixty or so stores and struggled to expand its collections. The arrival of Hedi Slimane as Creative Director in 2012, followed by Francesca Bellettini as President and CEO in 2013, marked a turning point. Then, a new era of creativity and growth for the House began with the appointment of Anthony Vaccarello as Creative Director in 2016. "From the very beginning, Anthony has embraced the legacy and embodied the attitude of Saint Laurent, recalls Francesca Bellettini. "Since he joined the House, Anthony has kept the brand relevant and compelling without ever compromising its legacy. Putting creativity at the center has been the essence of our strategy and the driver of our success." Between

Top: The Gucci store in Beverly Hills, California.
Bottom: The Gucci Valigeria store, opened in 2022, on Rue Saint-Honoré in Paris.

Top: Balenciaga's historic store at 10 Avenue George V, Paris.
Bottom: The Balenciaga store on New Bond Street, London.

2012 and 2022, the House experienced exceptional growth: the number of directly-owned stores grew from 89 to 280; during the same period, revenue jumped from 473 million to 3.3 billion euros.

The case of Bottega Veneta is equally exemplary of the evolution that the group's brands have undergone since their acquisition. When Kering took control in 2001, the Italian label had some twenty stores and revenue of 35 million euros. Twenty years later, thanks to the creative contributions of Tomas Maier, then Daniel Lee, and later Matthieu Blazy, it completely transformed in scale, with 263 stores and revenue of 1.5 billion euros.

Balenciaga experienced a similar transformation. When it was acquired by Kering in 2001, the brand's aura was prestigious but had been on a thirty-year hiatus since its founder, Cristóbal Balenciaga, had decided to retire from haute couture. Relaunched in 1997 under the artistic direction of Nicolas Ghesquière, it took on a new dimension when Isabelle Guichot was appointed to head the brand in 2007. The appointment of Demna Gvasalia as Artistic Director in 2015, with Cédric Charbit joining as President and CEO the following year, launched a new phase. While the designer completely rejuvenated the House's collections, the CEO expanded its horizons. "Balenciaga offered only women's ready-to-wear, accessories and shoes, and sneakers for men. So we were incredibly ambitious in developing the product categories, the men's line and, later, haute couture. We also expanded the number of stores quite considerably. Balenciaga had a wonderful, though little discussed, history, but its commercial reality was limited. Thus, we worked to develop the House and to strengthen its reputation so that it could become a global brand in step with its time," says Cédric Charbit. While the collections were undergoing a spectacular revival, its store network was developing rapidly, from 90 in 2014 to 247 in 2022.

By the end of the 2010s, on the eve of the Covid-19 pandemic, the Houses had lost none of their vitality. Today, their horizons continue to expand, including artistically. In June 2018, Daniel Lee took over as Artistic Director of Bottega Veneta. Previously ready-to-wear director for Celine, he was a virtual unknown in the world of fashion. The young designer immediately brought a fresh eye to the collections, which appealed to a younger clientele. The House simultaneously augmented its distribution network. An 800-square-meter flagship store opened in Tokyo, the brand's largest in Asia. A year later, in 2019, a new CEO, Bartolomeo Rongone, took over the helm. Formerly the Chief Operating Officer for Yves Saint Laurent, his focus was on reinvigorating the brand's potential while remaining true to its foundations. "From the moment I arrived, I was impressed by the brand's two founding principles. Craftsmanship and creativity are deeply rooted in its identity. Our original motto, 'Labor et Ingenium' (in English, Work and Talent), says a lot about Bottega Veneta's vision, which unlike other brands that work with a single designer, is borne of the shared passion of several artists. I have also seen how the brand has been building both a local and global identity since it began. It is deeply connected to the Veneto region—its architecture, colors, and craft traditions—while maintaining an unwavering commitment to international art and culture, such as the opening of our first store in New York in 1972 and our collaboration with Andy Warhol. Bottega Veneta has always shown a strong commitment to creative expression in all its forms and to excellence in craftsmanship," he explains today. In 2021, Bottega Veneta once again took the fashion world by surprise, announcing the appointment of Matthieu Blazy as Artistic

The facade and interior of the Alexander McQueen store
on Bond Street, London.

Director. As it had from 2010 to 2015, Kering embraced risk and bet on a figure little known to the general public.

In 2018 and again in 2019, propelled by the momentum of its Houses, Kering posted record results. The group was taking full advantage of the continued growth of the luxury market, and more particularly of the "Gucci rocket"—with thanks to the newspaper *Les Echos* for the expression—whose success with millennials was incontestable. Between 2018 and 2019, the group's revenue increased from 13.7 to 15.9 billion euros. A remarkable performance, driven primarily by the North American and Asian markets, which recorded growth of more than 30 percent. "Our performance is linked to our vision of modern luxury, with a clear focus on creativity, which allows us to grow beyond market trends," said François-Henri Pinault, commenting on the 2018 results. While these results owe much to the creativity, even the daring, that drive its various brands, they can also be explained by the pooling of support functions throughout the value chain. This integration strategy, which was first implemented in 2011, allowed the group to support its brands' rapid growth and enable them to focus on the essential: the creation of exceptional products. The sharing of expertise benefits functions related to raw material supplies, logistics, purchasing, legal services, career management, real estate, and information systems. This also held true in the digital field, which had been experiencing significant changes since 2018.

E-commerce: A time of reinternalization

The same year, Kering decided to reinternalize its e-commerce activities. Since 2012, these had been managed as part of a partnership with Yoox Net-a-Porter (YNAP), which had developed e-commerce sites for each of the group's brands with the exception of Gucci, which had remained autonomous in that regard. The collaboration had proved extremely successful, with the group's various Houses accessing the online Chinese market since 2013. However, by the end of 2018, the situation had changed significantly: while digital sales remained modest in relation to revenue, they were growing at a very sustained pace, averaging around 40 percent annually since 2015.

For Kering, the time had come to regain control of its digital resources, take advantage of online commerce's rapid growth, and maintain control of its image. It would also allow the group to better respond to client expectations and anticipate trends through collecting live data, which is why mastering the digital assets was so important. In late 2017, the group established a digital department. "Kering's digital vision was clear," says Grégory Boutté, Chief Client & Digital Officer. "It was related to both market evolution, with the emergence of a younger and highly connected clientele, particularly in China, and the convictions of the group's leaders. They saw digital tools as a way to enhance every stage of the value chain: production, distribution, and logistics. So the stakes were high."

Reinternalizing e-commerce meant ending the partnership with Yoox Net-a-Porter. This was a crucial step. Yoox had managed all the technical and logistical aspects of e-commerce, meaning Kering was dependent on a third party. However, according to some projections, by 2025 e-commerce would represent 25 percent of the luxury market. Therefore, it was essential for the group to take control of that distribution channel, and in particular to manage the customer experience. This is why luxury brands

Left: The Saint Laurent store on Boulevard Saint-Germain, Paris.
Right: The Saint Laurent Spring-Summer 2022 runway show at the Trocadéro in Paris.

focus on developing their own stores; the internalization of e-commerce meets the same demand. The approach would continue in stages until 2021. At the same time, the group was working to develop new professional applications, including with Apple, for example, to let in-store sales staff check stock status and know every customer's purchase history. The development of a voluntary digital strategy would soon lead the group to examine new business models.

Strengthening resources

To keep pace with the tremendous growth of the luxury market since the early 2010s, the group had also been strengthening its industrial resources.

At Gucci, a turning point came in April 2018 with the inauguration of the Gucci ArtLab, located in the Florentine commune of Scandicci. As Marco Bizzarri notes, this was one of Italy's largest industrial investments. And one of the most original: conceived as both a center of excellence for leather goods and footwear, and as an incubator for new ideas, ArtLab brings together all prototyping and manufacturing operations in 398,264 square feet (37,000 square meters). A first in the sector, ArtLab even has its own R&D center, which works with the brand's entire supply chain. This new kind of industrial platform has been central to Gucci for meeting increased demand.

In 2019, Kering Eyewear consolidated its supply chain with the opening of a new logistics center in Vescovana, in the Veneto region, a few kilometers from Villa Zaguri, the company's headquarters.

Opened in 2020, the new Kering global logistics center responds to demand from all the group's companies, whether orders are from the wholesale network, e-commerce sites, or regional warehouses. Completed in record time in Trecate, near Milan, it covers more than 1743,753 square feet (162,000 square meters) and can deliver 80 million pieces per year.

As the creation of the ArtLab and the logistics centers in Vescovana and Trecate attest, Italy more than ever played a decisive role in the group's organization and strategy. It was here, in 1999, that Kering began its transformation into a luxury pure player by taking a stake in Gucci. At the beginning of the 2020s, Italian brands—Gucci, Bottega Veneta, Brioni, Pomellato, and DoDo—represented almost half of the group's portfolio. The group employs more than 12,000 people in the peninsula, a quarter of its total workforce. It has twenty-eight production sites, including four tanneries. Even its French brands have headed to Italy. For example, Saint Laurent has a leather goods workshop in Scandicci, Tuscany, and produces its shoe collections in Vigonza, Veneto. In 2022, the company opened a new 28,000-square-meter leather goods workshop near Florence. As for Balenciaga, in 2021 the House inaugurated a leather goods factory in Cerreto Guidi, also near Florence. With several Italian nationals as members, the group's Executive Committee reflects Italy's importance. A country of unique expertise with world-renowned sectors of excellence, particularly for leatherwork and eyewear, Italy is a constant source of inspiration and creativity for Kering.

The group was also investing elsewhere in the world. In 2019, it strengthened its logistical capabilities in the United States by opening a new North American logistics hub in Wayne, New Jersey. With a surface area of 769,619 square feet (71,500 square meters), the site is certified "gold" level in the LEED (Leadership in Energy and Environmental Design) rating system. This state-of-the-art complex replaced Kering's former facilities in Secaucus and better accommodates the strong demand and ongoing growth of its various Houses' activities. On the other side of the world, in Japan, Kering inaugurated its new Tokyo headquarters in October 2020. It is situated in an iconic tower on Omotesando, where Gucci, Saint Laurent, Boucheron, and Balenciaga already have stores. The building is a showcase for the group in this historic and strategic market.

France, the group's birthplace, was not forgotten either. Kering has a number of sites across the country, including its headquarters on Rue de Sèvres, alongside those of Yves Saint Laurent, Balenciaga, and Boucheron. Saint Laurent's ready-to-wear atelier has long been in Angers—the brand is the only French ready-to-wear House to have its own atelier. In 2017, France Croco, a renowned French crocodile tannery acquired by Kering in 2013, based in Périers in the Manche region, moved to a brand-new site.

As for Kering Eyewear, a strategic agreement signed with Richemont in 2017 allowed it to change scale. Richemont, owner of Cartier, took a 30 percent stake in the company, and in exchange brought its eyewear activities and brands (including Cartier, Dunhill, and Montblanc) to Kering. As part of this partnership, Kering Eyewear also took over a factory dedicated to the manufacture of Cartier glasses located in Sucy-en-Brie, in the Val-de-Marne region.

By the early 2020s, the group had considerably expanded its industrial footprint. New workshops and logistics centers in Italy and the United States now enabled it to meet growing demand and distribute products more quickly around the world; Kering has offices in Paris, Milan, Florence, London, New York, Hong Kong, Shanghai, Tokyo, Seoul, Singapore, and other regions. This organization proved a crucial asset at a time when the Covid-19 pandemic threw everything into question.

"Maintaining activity, building the future"

Amidst its growth, Kering was taken by surprise when the Covid crisis hit in late 2019. In the months that followed, all the markets in which the group operated went into lockdown one after the other. By the end of April 2020, Europe, the United States, Latin America, Japan, and China had closed their borders and implemented stringent lockdown measures. The dates and lengths of these initiatives varied according to the country and health situation, which enabled Kering to mitigate the shock according to containment schedules, because its markets were never all closed at the same time. The crisis had a pronounced impact on the luxury sector's immediate horizon. The sudden closure of stores around the world and the collapse of tourism-related spending led to a sharp drop in sales for all players. No House was spared. Gucci's sales fell by 23 percent in 2020. To minimize the impact of the crisis, the group implemented cost-reduction plans for each House. Marketing campaigns were canceled or postponed, production was restricted, and stocks were reallocated to countries that were not yet affected or whose borders remained open.

The pandemic also forced Kering to reconsider its priorities. The first of these was protecting its employees. Supporting managers by establishing work-from-home policies, the mass distribution of masks, testing on

The Brioni store in London.

all sites, setting up medical video conferencing and a psychological assistance hotline: everything was put in place to ensure health and safety. The other priority was to help the Houses maintain their activity. To this end, the group increased its internal communications via messages, videos, and live events. This presence helped preserve the links between teams, encouraging employees to share advice on how to make the most of remote working.

The group also supported caregivers and frontline responders. In 2020, 15 million euros were donated, in the form of cash and medical equipment, to hospitals, civil protection organizations, Red Cross branches, and so on. Kering converted part of its production facilities in order to manufacture medical equipment. The Saint Laurent and Balenciaga workshops, as well as the Italian sites of Brioni and Gucci, produced certified masks and equipment. Even the group's logistics were called upon: thanks to these, three million masks from China were transported to French care units. "Kering is pronounced 'caring,' to take care," the group had explained when presenting its new identity in 2013. Kering had never been as true to its values as it was during those months of crisis.

The other priority was to adapt business to the new situation created by the pandemic. "While it was happening, we also had to guarantee the sustainability and continuity of our activities throughout our value chain and preserve the tens of thousands of direct and indirect jobs we generate, all without sacrificing our long-term trajectory, our vision, and our convictions," Jean-François Palus says today. The flexibility and responsiveness characteristic of the group proved to be major assets. Faced with unprecedented challenges, Kering was adapting, experimenting with new solutions, and transforming its organization. For example, following the cancellation of the Watches and Wonders show, Ulysse Nardin and Girard-Perregaux, in association with fifteen other watch manufacturers, created Geneva Watch Days, a self-managed, multi-brand show that allowed them to unveil new collections; to make up for the cancellation of Milan Fashion Week—a key event in the fashion calendar—in 2020, Kering's various Houses, with support from the group's technical teams, mounted virtual showrooms in a matter of weeks. Similarly, to enable sales staff to maintain a connection with their customers, solutions for sales and payments were widely implemented. At a time when physical stores were closed, e-commerce was essential to driving the group's business.

Coincidentally, the Covid crisis came at a time when brands' e-commerce sites—previously managed in partnership with Yoox Net-a-Porter—were being rapidly transferred to the group's platform. This made it possible to rapidly implement new functionalities and smoother, more efficient, indeed innovative, digital experiences. The development of e-commerce also involved strengthening the online presence of the group's various brands in major luxury markets, beginning with China. Emblematic of this, the partnership that Gucci, Boucheron, and Alexander McQueen signed in December 2020 with the Chinese platform Tmall Luxury Pavilion, owned by the Alibaba group, resulted in the opening of virtual stores. From that point on, 750 million consumers would have access to those three brands.

At the end of 2020, when the time came for the initial assessment, Kering was able to look to the future with optimism. Although results decreased, as was the case for all luxury players, the group's model and strategy were uncompromised. In a difficult situation, it had managed, as it says, "to maintain its activity while laying a solid foundation to build the future." In particular, the group benefited from the faster-than-expected recovery of certain markets, particularly China. In the spring of 2020, it was able to reopen most of its stores in Mainland China and welcome a clientele that, although they could no longer travel, were just as interested in luxury products. E-commerce played a fundamental role in the group's resilience during the Covid crisis. In 2021, it represented 12 percent of the group's total sales, compared to 4.7 percent three years earlier. The industrial organization implemented by the group has, in the same way, also proved a key asset. Becoming operational just before or at the beginning of the pandemic, the new logistics centers have enabled the group to efficiently respond to demand from e-commerce sites and stores that were open. And, thanks to its locations around the world, the group has been able to concentrate on local clientele, who, unable to travel, have accounted for most of its business. At a time when the crisis is receding and the market is beginning to show strong signs of recovery, Kering has all the resources in place to return to growth.

Recovery

From the last quarter of 2020, recovery became noticeable, varying in different countries and geographical areas, with that of luxury accelerating in 2021 and remaining stable the following year, despite uncertainties caused by the Chinese government's "zero Covid" policy. In 2021, Kering even announced record results, with revenue of 17.6 billion euros, up 35 percent compared to 2020, which of course was a very particular year, but also significantly higher than that of 2019. As before the Covid crisis, organic growth and the consolidation of the companies' joint growth platforms remain the strategic guidelines that Kering intends to follow. While the Houses focus on what is essential to them—creative energy, excellence in craftsmanship, customer relations, communications, etc.—the group continues to pool resources around a number of shared functions. The completion of the Trecate logistics hub in 2021 is aligned with this strategy. So, too, is the continued internalization of e-commerce platforms, completed in 2021 with the integration of the Balenciaga and Bottega Veneta sites.

The priority given to organic growth was also reflected in a strengthening of the group's control over its distribution and the consequent reduction in third-party distributors. The opening of directly-owned stores, which slowed down during the Covid crisis, began accelerating again in 2021. That year, Bottega Veneta opened new addresses on Omotesando in Tokyo, Via Condotti in Rome, and in New York's SoHo district. The company now had a network of 263 stores around the world. For its part, Saint Laurent opened twenty-nine stores, including nine in Greater China. Qeelin also expanded its presence in China, with six new stores, plus one in Singapore, while Boucheron continued to strengthen its presence in Asia. With tourist numbers struggling to pick up again, especially among travelers from China, the objective was to serve Chinese customers in their home market.

At the same time, the group continued rationalizing its brand portfolio with the January 2022 sale of the two Swiss watchmaking brands Girard-Perregaux and Ulysse Nardin to their management. With this deal, Kering withdrew from watchmaking, a sector in which its presence had remained modest and its growth prospects limited. This operation was part of the strategy of "giving priority to the Houses with the potential to become sizable assets within the group, and to which it can provide decisive support over time." Kering was, however, maintaining its increasingly buoyant jewelry business, embodied by Boucheron, Pomellato, and Qeelin, which had been experiencing dynamic growth for several years.

Boucheron symbolically reopened its historic Place Vendôme store, the Hôtel de Nocé, in December 2018 following an extensive renovation. Recognized for its expertise, the House is also distinguished by its creative vision, led by Claire Choisne, Creative Director since 2011, and exemplified in twice-yearly collections of high jewelry. The first, "Histoire de Style," freely reinterprets the House's archives; the second, "Carte Blanche," is imbued with an audacious approach to innovation. Capitalizing on the success of the iconic *Quatre* collection, the company continues to gradually strengthen its international presence, particularly in Asia and the Middle East.

Pomellato, though younger, has also experienced remarkable growth by launching in new territories, particularly in Asia. In 2020, it took a major step, presenting its first high jewelry collection, *La Gioia*. The 165 pieces designed by Vincenzo Castaldo, Pomellato's Artistic Director, were in part inspired by the archives of the House, which was founded in Milan in 1967, as well as its most popular designs: the *Nudo* rings, *Tango* chains, and *Ritratto* hard stones.

In 2019, Qeelin made another decisive move, becoming the first Chinese jeweler on the prestigious Place Vendôme in Paris. A highly symbolic step for the brand, which has been experiencing phenomenal growth in China.

In the months following the pandemic, the group began organizing itself to take full advantage of the luxury market's growth potential. At the same time, the Houses continued to reinvent, create, and surprise. In this regard, the Covid crisis has acted as an "innovation accelerator," forcing people to think outside the box and imagine new solutions to deal with emerging market constraints or trends. This was how Balenciaga, to mention just one example, played a very original card. During the presentation of its fall 2021 collection, the brand invented a new kind of fashion show, in this case a video game accessible in virtual reality. This was a first in the world of fashion. The House's Spring-Summer 2022 collection also stood apart by creating a new episode of *The Simpsons*, whose characters walked the runway in front of prestigious guests.

Gucci, for its part, opened a new chapter in its history: in January 2023, the brand announced Sabato De Sarno as its new Creative Director. Like his predecessor, the thirty-nine-year-old Italian was not well known by the general public but had a good reputation among fashion insiders. At just 102 years old, the Florentine House is determined to remain at the forefront of creativity and craftsmanship.

When the recovery began, the group's leaders announced that, "Priority is being given to organic growth," though they specified that "this will not, however, prevent necessary acquisitions." In fact, at the end of the pandemic, the group was undertaking acquisitions, particularly for Kering Eyewear. In July 2021, it took control of Danish luxury eyewear manufacturer Lindberg, adding a sixteenth brand to its portfolio. Another followed in October 2022, this time with Maui Jim, created in Hawaii in 1987, which had become one of the world's leading brands of high-end sunglasses. These acquisitions are indicative of the group's strategy: to seize opportunities to strengthen itself as they arise in various markets. But that's not all. Faithful to the entrepreneurial spirit that has driven the company since its creation and eager to always be at the vanguard of innovation in order to anticipate

Top: Casa Pomellato, the jeweler's headquarters in Milan, Italy.
Bottom: The Pomellato store in Rome, Italy.

In 2021, Kering Eyewear announced the acquisition of Danish luxury eyewear manufacturer
Lindberg; it was followed by that of Maui Jim, an American brand of high-end sunglasses, in 2022.

consumer expectations, it also intends to explore new territories and new business models.

At the vanguard of innovation

To pioneer innovation, the group created Kering Ventures, a dedicated structure through which it can test emerging ideas and new models by investing in promising start-ups. In this way, it can keep pace with new trends and experiment with innovative practices before potentially adopting them.

In March 2021, Kering took part, along with other investors, in financing launched by Vestiaire Collective. Founded in 2009, the French resale specialist has become the world's leading platform in second-hand luxury. Driven by the younger generations' growing ecological commitment and the expansion of online commerce, the market in which it operates is flourishing, especially since the Covid-19 pandemic. By participating in Vestiaire Collective's fundraising, which ensured Kering a 5 percent stake in its capital, the group is betting on an innovative business model, one aimed at younger generations of consumers in particular.

The same objective was behind the group's acquisition of a stake in the London-based handbag rental specialist Cocoon. Created in 2019, the start-up supplies its customers, via a subscription service, with luxury bags from more than thirty brands. Like the second-hand market, the luxury goods rental market is another niche the group intends to explore. Taking into consideration the habits of young consumers, the group in September 2021 participated in fundraising for the American live shopping platform NTWRK. In each case, the goal is to take a minority stake in start-ups developing disruptive experiences and services for the next generation of luxury clients.

Other deals will certainly follow. Since 2022, Kering has been interested in disruptive technologies connected to Web3 and the metaverse—innovations that are likely to revolutionize the luxury industry. Nothing could be more natural: throughout its history, the group has reinvented itself, challenged convention, and anticipated new practices to seize or create growth opportunities. Sixty years after its creation, its energy, determination, and agility remain as strong as ever.

Top: Kering's global logistics center in Trecate, Italy.
Bottom: The offices of Kering's American logistics center in Wayne, New Jersey.
Pages 236-237: In 1893, Boucheron became the first high jewelry House
to open a store on the Place Vendôme in Paris, in the Hôtel de Nocé.

Peter Fischli and David Weiss, *Untitled (Rock on Top of Another Rock, for Dinard)*, 2013–14.
Stone, 220¹⁵/₃₂ × 118⁷/₆₄ × 118⁷/₆₄ in. (560 × 300 × 300 cm), Pinault Collection.

THE GREAT ENTREPRENEURIAL ADVENTURE ...

Six employees and 600,000 francs in revenue (the equivalent of just over 930,000 euros) in the first year and, sixty years later, 47,000 employees and revenue of more than 20 billion euros. A magnificent adventure: created in Brittany in 1962, the Kering group has become over the course of its often-surprising history the world's second-largest luxury company. The key to this amazing success story, above anything else, is an entrepreneurial spirit. Instilled from the beginning by the group's founder, François Pinault, it continues to inspire his son and successor, François-Henri Pinault. The determination and appetite for entrepreneurship, with daring and a flair for risk, are the essence of the group's identity. In 1962, an entrepreneurial spirit convinced François Pinault to leave a promising professional situation to open his own timber business, the starting point of his incredible ascent. While still young and inconsequential in the eyes of his competitors, it was also that spirit that led him to wage a triumphant battle against the powerful corporation of timber importers that controlled the market, and, in the early 1990s, to seize new opportunities and transition into retail and distribution, and then — to everyone's surprise — to create a Luxury division. It was this same entrepreneurial spirit that, from 2003, led François-Henri Pinault to progressively withdraw from retail and distribution to build one of the world's leaders in luxury. While the group has never stopped transforming and evolving its business model—first timber and then retail and distribution, and finally, luxury—at every stage in its development, it has shown astounding flexibility and remarkable reactivity, always acting with calculated daring and guided by a potent entrepreneurial culture. This is still what drives Kering to innovate, to explore new territories, and to push the frontiers of luxury ever further. The entrepreneurial spirit is the thread that runs through the group's history, which began over sixty years ago in Rennes.

This thread has its origins in the group's family dimension. This is without doubt the other secret to Kering's remarkable success. Since its very beginnings, the group has been controlled and directed by the founding family. In sixty years, it has known only two leaders, who share the same entrepreneurial spirit and the same flair for risk: François and François-Henri Pinault. Remarkable consistency! Although they have surrounded themselves with experienced managers and many talented people who have all played, and continue to play, key roles in the group's development, the Pinaults remain the soul of Kering, and their vision the foundation of its strategic directions. Far from being anonymous, Kering is fully personified. This is one of its strengths and the guarantee of a long-term perspective.

The family is also the primary source of the values that have guided the group since its beginnings, which François-Henri Pinault often evokes: daring, creativity, trust, responsibility, loyalty, tenacity, and vigilance. These are the other threads running through Kering's history. They have also shaped human relationships within the group. Empathy, and respect for others, for their integrity and dignity, permeate Kering today and inspire everything it does.

An entrepreneurial spirit, family, and the values they impart: these are the pillars of Kering, as solid as granite. But that history is also one of imagination and dreams. It is its capacity to imagine new business models that has enabled the group to question and reinvent itself, seize opportunities, and explore new territories. Today, it is driven by one ambition: to shape the luxury industry of tomorrow. It is upon this vision that Kering's auspicious future will be built. Since 1962, Kering has been built on granite and dreams, the same materials that will undoubtedly pave the way for its future.

THE
HOUSES

1921
Guccio Gucci founds the House
in Florence, Italy

1999
The House joins the Kering group

GUCCI

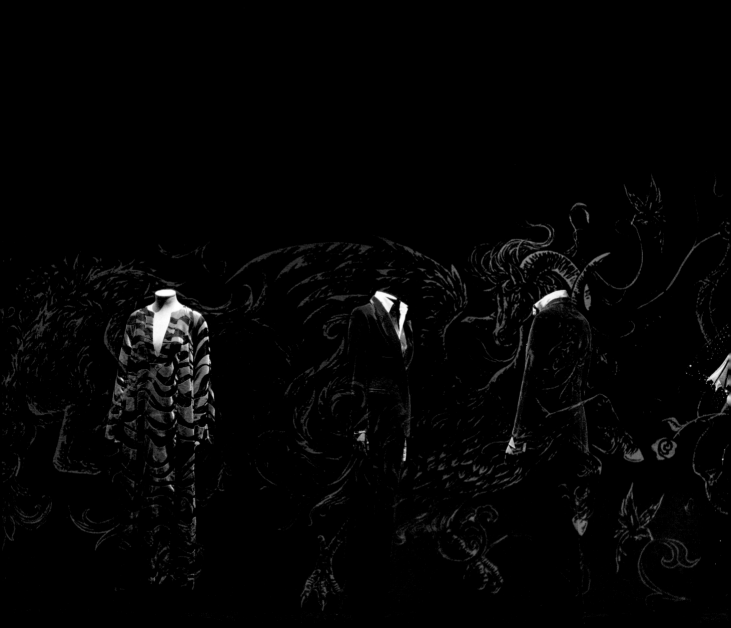

1961

Yves Saint Laurent founds
the House in Paris, France

1999

The House joins the Kering group

SAINT
LAURENT

from Y. S. L.
Amicalement A. M. C.
62

1966

Michele Taddei and Renzo Zengario found
the House in Vicenza, Italy

2001

The House joins the Kering group

BOTTEGA VENETA

When
your
own
initials
are
enough

BOTTEGA VENETA

1917
Cristóbal Balenciaga founds
the House in San Sebastián, Spain

2001
The House joins the Kering group

BALENCIAGA

1992

Lee Alexander McQueen founds
the House in London, England

2001

The House joins the Kering group

ALEXANDER McQUEEN

1945

Nazareno Fonticoli and Gaetano Savini
found the House in Rome, Italy

2012

The House joins the Kering group

BRIONI

1858
Frédéric Boucheron founds
the House in Paris, France

1999
The House joins the Kering group

BOUCHERON

BOUCHERON

JOAILLIER

NEW-YORK   PARIS   LONDRES

BOUCHERON

JOAILLIER — 26, PLACE VENDOME — PARIS

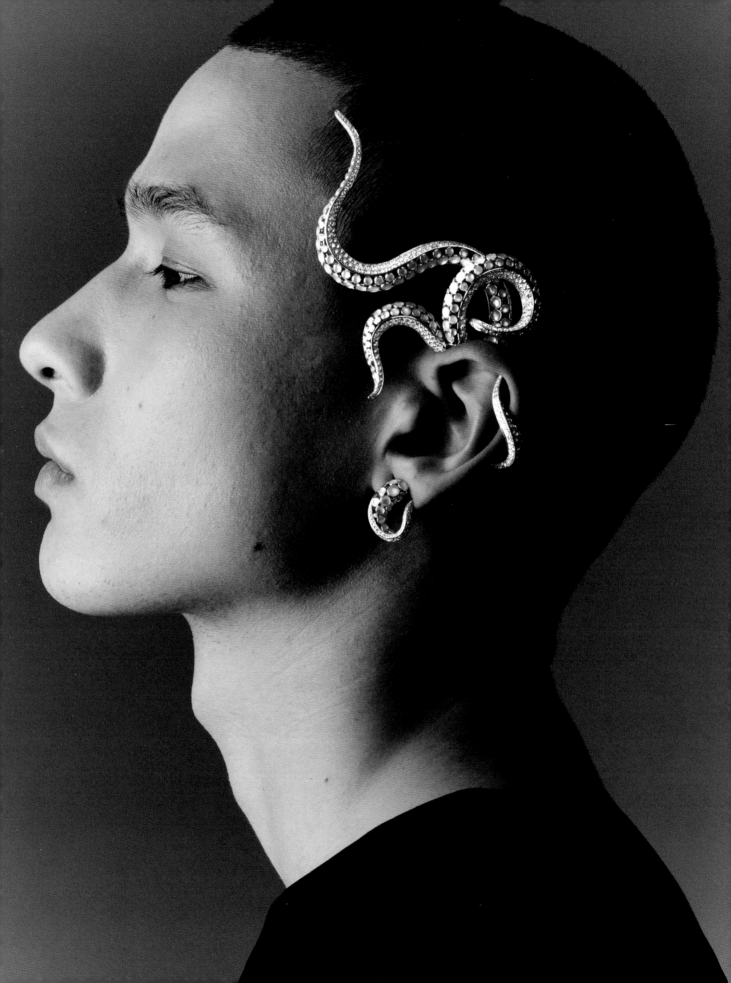

1967
Pino Rabolini founds the House in Milan, Italy

2013
The House joins the Kering group

POMELLATO

2004
Dennis Chan founds the House
in Hong Kong, China

2013
The House joins the Kering group

QEELIN

2015
Creation of Kering Eyewear

KERING EYEWEAR

EMPOWERING

IMAGINATION

GUCCI

p. 1: Brigitte Bardot wearing the iconic Gucci horsebit loafers in Deauville, 1968; photographed by Terry O'Neill © Terry O'Neill/Iconic Images
p. 2: Samuel Beckett carrying a Gucci bag, photographed by Lucio Berzioli in 1971 © Photo12/Alamy/Farabola
pp. 3–4: *Gucci Cosmos* exhibition, Shanghai, 2023 © Gucci

SAINT LAURENT

p. 1: Model wearing the iconic Yves Saint Laurent tuxedo, photographed on Rue Aubriot in Paris, 1975 © Helmut Newton Foundation/Trunk Archive
p. 2: Logo designed by Cassandre for Yves Saint Laurent in 1961 © Yves Saint Laurent/A. M. Mouron- Cassandre
p. 3: Awar and Freja, Fall-Winter 2022 by Anthony Vaccarello © Juergen Teller
p. 4: Marilou, Spring-Summer 2023 by Anthony Vaccarello © Juergen Teller

BOTTEGA VENETA

p. 1: Lauren Hutton in the film *American Gigolo* by Paul Schrader, 1980 © Photo12/Alamy/Landmark Media/Paramount Pictures
p. 2: Bottega Veneta advertising campaign, 1970s © Kenyon Anderson
p. 3: Bottega Veneta advertising campaign © Malick Bodian/Second Name Agency
p. 4: Kate Moss for Bottega Veneta, Spring-Summer 2023 campaign © Sander/254forest

BALENCIAGA

p. 1: "Le Chou Noir" evening cape, Winter 1967 © Archives Balenciaga Paris, photo Jean Kublin
p. 2: Wedding dress, Summer 1967 © Archives Balenciaga Paris, photo Jean Kublin
p. 3: Fall-Winter 2016 collection, courtesy of Balenciaga
p. 4: Danielle Slavik, Couture collection 2022, courtesy of Balenciaga

ALEXANDER McQUEEN

pp. 1–2: Alexander McQueen Spring-Summer 1999 runway show © Victor Virgile/Gamma-Rapho
p. 3: *Anatomy*, Fall-Winter 2023 collection © InDigital
p. 4: Fall-Winter 2019 collection © Jet Swan

BRIONI

p. 1: The first men's runway show in history, organized by Brioni in 1952 at Palazzo Pitti in Florence; courtesy of Brioni
p. 2: Gaetano Savini, one of the House's two founders, adjusting a suit in front of the Brioni store on the Via Barberini in Rome, in the 1950s; courtesy of Brioni
p. 3: Anthony Hopkins for Brioni © Gregory Harris/MA+Group
p. 4: Jude Law for Brioni © Annemarieke van Drimmelen/MA+Group

BOUCHERON

p. 1: Advertisement in the magazine *Plaisir de France*, 1946 © Archives Boucheron
p. 2: Advertisement in *Vogue*, 1966 © Archives Boucheron
p. 3: Earring from the "Volcano Man" parure, part of the "Carte Blanche – Ailleurs" high jewelry collection, 2022 © Boucheron
p. 4: Three "New Maharani" necklaces created for the "History of Style – New Maharajahs" high jewelry collection, 2022 © Boucheron

POMELLATO

pp. 1–2: Lilly Bistrattin for Pomellato, Milan, 1971 © Gian Paolo Barbieri/Courtesy of Fondazione Gian Paolo Barbieri
p. 3: Benedetta Porcaroli for Pomellato © Gregory Harris/MA+Group
p. 4: Larissa Hofmann and Helen Nonini © Peter Lindbergh/Peter Lindbergh Foundation

QEELIN

pp. 1, 3, 4: © Qeelin
p. 2: The Qeelin store on Place Vendôme in Paris © Éric Sander

KERING EYEWEAR

pp. 1–2: Villa Zaguri, the headquarters of Kering Eyewear, near Padua, Italy © Kering Eyewear
p. 3: Maui Jim campaign © Kering Eyewear
p. 4: Lindberg campaign © Kering Eyewear

CAPTIONS AND CREDITS. LAENNEC PORTFOLIO

p. 144: (t) Laennec Hospital, Rue de Sèvres, c. 1900 © Léon et Lévy/Roger-Viollet; (cl) The Saint-François courtyard, 1869–1902 © Pierre Emonts/Musée Carnavalet/ Roger-Viollet; (cr) The main courtyard, c. 1900 © BIU Santé, Paris; (bl) The chapel and radiating chapel, between 1869 and 1902 © Pierre Emonts/ Musée Carnavalet/Roger-Viollet ; (br) The sundial, Gamard courtyard, between 1869 and 1902 © Pierre Emonts/ Musée Carnavalet/ Roger-Viollet.
p. 146: Illustration © Pierre Le-Tan, 2017
pp. 147, 150, 151, 152, 153: © Sophie Alyz
pp. 148–49, 156–57: © Thierry Depagne
pp. 154, 155: © Éric Sander

pp. 158–59
Échos, European Heritage Days 2016, Laennec chapel, Paris, photo © Diane Arques/Adagp, Paris, 2023

Left
Hiroshi Sugimoto, *The Last Supper*, 1999
Black and white gelatin silver prints
59½ × 291 × 3⅛ in. (151.13 × 739.14 × 8 cm)
Pinault Collection
© Hiroshi Sugimoto

At the back, on the wall
Andres Serrano, *Black Supper*, 1991
Five Cibachrome prints face mounted on Plexiglas
45 × 168 in. (114.3 × 426.7 cm)
Pinault Collection
© Andres Serrano

At the back, on the floor
Maurizio Cattelan, *All*, 2007
Nine white Carrara marble sculptures
Installation, variable dimensions
Pinault Collection
© Maurizio Cattelan

Right
Adel Abdessemed, *Décor*, 2011–12
Razor wire
Installation, variable dimensions
Pinault Collection
© Adel Abdessemed/Adagp, Paris, 2023

pp. 160–61
Faire Avec, European Heritage Days 2017, Laennec chapel, Paris, photo © Diane Arques/Adagp, Paris, 2023

Left
El Anatsui, *New Layout*, 2009
Liquor bottle caps and copper wire
88³⁷⁄₆₄ × 119⁹⁄₆₄ × 5²⁹⁄₃₂ in. (225 × 303 × 15 cm)
© El Anatsui
Courtesy of the artist and Jack Shainman Gallery, New York.

Back
Subodh Gupta, *Very Hungry God*, 2006
Stainless steel structure covered in around 3,000 steel cooking utensils and polished steel
153³⁵⁄₆₄ × 125⁶³⁄₆₄ × 157³¹⁄₆₄ in. (390 × 320 × 400 cm)
Pinault Collection
© Subodh Gupta

Right
El Anatsui, *Depletion*, 2009
Aluminum and copper wire
115¾ × 370⁵⁵⁄₆₄ × 5²⁹⁄₃₂ in. (294 × 942 × 15 cm)
Pinault Collection
© El Anatsui
Courtesy of the artist and Jack Shainman Gallery, New York.

pp. 162–63
Reliquaires, European Heritage Days 2018, Chapelle Laennec, Paris, photo © Éric Sander

Left
Günther Uecker, *Phantom Weiss I (White Phantom I)*, *Phantom Weiss II (White Phantom II)*, *Phantom Weiss III (White Phantom III)*, 2012
Nails and white paint with glue on canvas on wood
Overall dimensions (approx.):
78¾ × 177³⁄₁₆ in. (200 × 450 cm)
Pinault Collection
© Günther Uecker/Adagp, Paris, 2023

Center, foreground
James Lee Byars, *The Philosophical Nail*, 1986
Gilded iron
5 29/32 × 1 3/16 × 1 3/16 in.(27 × 3 × 3 cm)
Pinault Collection
© The Estate of the Artist

Center, background
James Lee Byars, *The Golden Tower*, 1974
Gilded column
71 × 19 3/4 × 19 3/4 × 21 5/8 in.
(180.34 × 50.17 × 50.17 × 55 cm)
Pinault Collection
© The Estate of the Artist

Background
James Lee Byars, *Byars Is Elephant*, 1997
Installation: rope and golden fabric
Installation, variable dimensions
Pinault Collection
© The Estate of the Artist

Right
Damien Hirst, *Jacob's Ladder*, 2008
Glass, stainless steel, steel, aluminum, nickel,
cork, and entomological specimens
92 15/16 × 342 1/2 × 4 13/16 in. (236 × 870 × 12.3 cm)
Pinault Collection
© Damien Hirst and Science Ltd./All rights
reserved, Adagp, Paris, 2023

pp. 164–65
Pleurs de joie, European Heritage Days 2019,
Chapelle Laennec, Kering headquarters, Paris,
photo © Éric Sander

Left
Sigmar Polke, *Zirkusfiguren*
(Circus Figures), 2005
Acrylic, artificial resin, and clay on fabric
118 1/8 × 196 7/8 in. (300 × 500 cm)
Pinault Collection
© The Estate of Sigmar Polke, Cologne/Adagp,
Paris, 2023

Foreground, left
Damien Hirst, *Mickey*, 2016
Bronze
35 13/16 × 27 15/16 × 24 in.(91 × 71 × 61 cm)
Pinault Collection
© Damien Hirst and Science Ltd./All rights
reserved, Adagp, Paris, 2023

Background, left
Damien Hirst, *The Collector with Friend*, 2016
Bronze
73 × 48 5/8 × 28 11/16 in. (185.42 × 123.44 × 72.9 cm)
Pinault Collection
© Damien Hirst and Science Ltd./All rights
reserved, Adagp, Paris, 2023

Center, background
Martial Raysse, *Noon Mediterranean Landscape*,
1966
Photographic technique, collage, acrylic,
flocking on canvas, and neon tube on Plexiglas
79 15/16 × 75 9/16 × 3 15/16 in. (203 × 192 × 10 cm)
Pinault Collection
© Martial Raysse/Adagp, Paris, 2023

Right
Sigmar Polke, *Die Trennung des Mondes von*
den einzelnen Planeten (Separating the Moon
from Each of the Planets), 2005
Acrylic and artificial resin on fabric
118 1/8 × 196 7/8 in. (300 × 500 cm)
Pinault Collection
© The Estate of Sigmar Polke, Cologne/
Adagp, Paris, 2023

pp. 166–67
Paysages, European Heritage Days 2021,
Chapelle Laennec, Kering headquarters, Paris,
photo © Éric Sander

Left
Hélène Delprat, *Ce que le Chevalier couvert*
de cendres a raconté à son retour, 2015
Pigment and acrylic on canvas, mounted
on a stretcher
102 9/16 × 341 47/64 in. (260.5 × 868 cm)
Pinault Collection
© Hélène Delprat/Adagp, Paris, 2023

Background
Paul Rebeyrolle, *Végas del condado
(Paysage espagnol)*, *Grands paysages* series, 1978
Painting on canvas
179 9/64 × 202 3/4 in. (455 × 515 cm)
Pinault Collection
© Paul Rebeyrolle/Adagp, Paris, 2023

Right
Hélène Delprat, *Où l'on découvre des merveilles
hydrauliques et bizarres*, 2016
Pigment and acrylic on canvas,
mounted on a stretcher
96 x 385 1/2 in. (246 × 979 cm)
Pinault Collection
© Hélène Delprat/Adagp, Paris, 2023

pp. 168–69
Aria of Inertia, European Heritage Days 2022,
Chapelle Laennec, Kering headquarters, Paris,
photo © Diane Arques/Adagp, Paris, 2023

On the floor, in the center
Edith Dekyndt, *Visitation Zone*, 2020
Installation: choregraphy, vivariums,
fluorescent tubes, and brined apples.
Commissioned by the Riga International
Biennial of Contemporary Art with the support
of the VV Foundation and the Riga Zoo.
Installation, variable dimensions.
Collection of the artist

Center, background
Edith Dekyndt, *Underground
(Le Val Saint-Germain)*, 2022
Cotton canvas, soil, and vegetation sediment
248 1/32 × 275 19/32 in.(630 × 700 cm)
Pinault Collection

Right
Edith Dekyndt, *Scrunch*, 2022
Broken glass embroidered on velvet
84 1/4 × 69 19/64 in. (214 × 176 cm)
Pinault Collection

pp. 170–71
Thomas Houseago's work *Study for Owl II*,
Kering headquarters
photo © Sophie Alyz

Thomas Houseago, *Study for Owl II*, 2011
Tuf-cal, hemp, and iron rebar
74 1/64 × 35 3/64 × 35 3/64 in. (188 × 89 × 89 cm)
Pinault Collection
© Thomas Houseago/Adagp, Paris, 2023

pp. 172-173
Balenciaga displays cotton toiles
—a fundamental step in the process of creating
a garment—in the exhibition *Cristóbal
Balenciaga: Le couturier sculpteur*, presented
during the 2019 European Heritage Days.
Taken from the House's archives, the pieces
are hand-annotated by the founder himself.
Photo © Éric Sander

p. 174: © Maud Rémy-Lonvis
p. 175: Illustration © Pierre Le-Tan, 2019

PHOTO CREDITS

ACKNOWLEDGMENTS

For their contributions, Kering would like to particularly thank:

Jean-Jacques Aillagon, Francesca Bellettini, Marco Bizzarri, Pierre Blayau, Grégory Boutté, Carlo Capasa, Cédric Charbit, Dominique de Charrin, Laurent Claquin, Bernard Compagnon, Jean-Michel Darrois, Marie-Claire Daveu, Stephen Decam, Philippe Decressac, Françoise Dévé, Annie-Claude Ducommun, Jean-Marc Duplaix, Valérie Duport, Mercedes Erra, Thierry Falque-Pierrotin, Jane Fonda, Michel Friocourt, Franz-Olivier Giesbert, Isabelle Guichot, Hubert Guidal, Patrick Guillot, Bethann Hardison, Ghada Hatem, François Henrot, Valérie Hermann, Hung Huang, Odile de Labouchère, Emma Lavigne, Béatrice Lazat, Bernard-Henri Lévy, Gilles Linard, Jean-Michel Mary, Anne Méaux, Alain Minc, Anne Mottu, Jean-François Palus, Paul Polman, Nazanine Ravaï, Julie Redon, Patricia Roger-Gallet, Xavier Romatet, Bartolomeo Rongone, Roberto Vedovotto, Alain Viry, Patrick de Vismes, Serge Weinberg, Jean-Luc Winter, and Anna Wintour.

Kering would also like to warmly thank the group's communications teams and the Houses for their invaluable help in producing this book.

KERING

Editors
Valérie Duport and Paul Michon
Editorial Direction
Didier Cazelles
Image Research Coordination
Bérengère Gaucher and Alice Maine
Project Coordination
Kate Shone, Élodie Rakotonirina

Historical Research
Hélène de Champchesnel, Historien-Conseil

Texts
Tristan Gaston-Breton

FLAMMARION

This book was produced by Flammarion's Editorial Partnerships Department.

Head of Partnerships
Henri Julien
Project Coordinator
Mathilde Jouret
Editorial Coordination
Geneviève de La Bretesche
Artistic Direction and Design
Agnès Dahan Studio,
Agnès Dahan and Baptiste Bignon
Picture Research
Pascale Dubreuil
Translation from French
Bronwyn Mahoney
Copyediting
Nom de Plume
Production
Corinne Trovarelli
Color Separation
Les Artisans du Regard, Paris

24 25 26 3 2 1

ISBN: 978-2-08-042814-1

Legal Deposit: 02/2024

Printed in Italy by Verona Libri, in October 2023